Poems From The Heart

Carol J. Hagan

May God Bless,
love,
Carol Hagan

I held the pencil; God gave me the words- Carol J. Hagan

DEDICATION

I would like to dedicate this book to the people who have made me who I am today. They include my parents, Bernice and Tommy Hagan; my daughter Taylor; my niece and nephew Mandy and Chris; my brothers Ricky and Robbie and several co-workers including Jessica, Belinda, Sherri, Cindy, and JoAnn. May this book touch your heart.

So Many Questions, Very Few Answers

Why do todays so called "mothers" opt to kill their innocent kids?
Why don't parents raise their children, like my parents always did?
Why are teenagers of today, so rebellious and run away?
Why do many people steal just to survive from day to day?

Why does a grown man choose to rape a little girl?
Why is there so much evilness throughout the entire world?
Why does a daddy desire to leave his wife and family?
Why don't people all over the world have plenty of food to eat?

Why does any given lawyer defend a guilty man?
Why so many whys, sometimes it's hard to understand?
Why do some nurses, lack compassion, kindness and care?
Why do people not believe, in either God or prayer?

Why do too many people only care about themselves?
When people are wrong, why do they blame it on someone else?
Why are some kids born with birth defects and cancer?
Maybe one day in the future, we'll know all of these answers.

Why are people always so quick and eager to judge?
Why do folks live each day with a lifelong grudge?
Why are little children bullies and not remorseful for words they say?
Why don't kids behave like they did in my younger days?

Why does a teenage girl walk a few blocks to meet a friend?
It never crossed her mind she wouldn't be seen alive again.
Why don't parents take the time to teach their kids right from wrong?
 I'll know all of this and more, when I ask the Man on the throne.

Holidays

I can't call you on New Year's at midnight, like all the years before,
Valentines to you now, is just a heart taped on your door.
Easter is not the same, since you're not at church at 6 am,
Smiling, sitting on the pew, clapping and saying Amen.

Mother's Day of all the days, I'm not so sure that you understand,
The day that's celebrated all over, for mothers throughout the land.
Memorial Day just comes and goes, with not much going on,
No holidays just aren't the same, since you're no longer home.

We try hard to celebrate Father's Day but you're not there by his side,
And when you're not with him, somehow it don't feel right.
Labor Day we just go to work, it seems to help pass the time,
Of better days we shared together, those memories now cloud your mind.

The Fourth of July, no fireworks do we watch as the skies light up,
We never have those cookouts, parties, good times and such.
Halloween we don't hand out candy for all the witches and goblins to eat,
I can't recall the last time I heard, a child say "Trick or Treat".

On Thanksgiving we still give thanks but we just go through the motions,
Sadly all we have now is a families' heart that's broken.
Christmas oh Christmas, the most dreaded holiday of all,
When I say "Merry Christmas", you just stare at the wall.

I never realized that holidays, could make me feel this way,
Once again I ask God for strength, when I bow my head to pray.
Never take holidays for granted, they're not the same unless all is there,
The excitement has now been replaced, with depression and despair.

I detest that word called "Alzheimer's", it can rip ones world apart,
And to the families that's going through this, I pray God touches your heart.
He alone is what carries me, when it seems I can't go on,
He sees my tears and weakness, when others think I'm oh so strong.

I Owe You

You know I actually owe you, for the very first breath of life,
No matter the pain that you were in, your concern was that I was alright.
I owe you for the discipline, yes all of those spankings too,
I owe you for teaching me so many things that later in life I'd need to do.

I owe you for all the meals you cooked and yes, yours were the best,
I owe you for making me study, so I could pass each test.
I owe you for my manners, making me say "yes sir" and no" ma'am" ,
I owe you for making me, everything that today I now am.

I owe you for the endless laundry, all my clothes you washed for years,
I owe you for always calming, each of my childhood fears.
I owe you for your guidance and teaching me right from wrong,
I owe you for your words of wisdom, especially now that I'm grown.

I owe you for always making me clean the house spic and span,
Saying cleanliness was next to Godliness, at the time I didn't understand.
I owe you for making me go to work, when I was very, very young,
It surely paid off in the long run, you can now ask anyone.

I owe you for dragging me to church, making me go to Sunday school,
Enforcing to me so strongly, to always follow the golden rule.
I owe you for the compassion and teaching me not to lie,
I owe you for the many times, you wiped my tears when I cried.

I owe you for mostly going without, so I could have things I seem to need,
I owe you for teaching me, to live life always doing good deeds.
I owe you for the countless times, you prayed for me each night,
I owe you for staying on your knees, just so I'd turn out just right.

I owe you for always listening, to every problem I thought I had,
And for making me realize, that the good always outweighs the bad.
I owe you for years of guidance, indeed I was guided by the best,
I owe you for always making me, appreciate things that I possess.

I owe you for the many times, you proved to be my very best friend,
I owe you for everything you did for me, with a love that will never end.
I owe you for all you instilled in me, that no one can take away,
And no matter how hard I try, this is a debt I could never repay.

Only A Mother

Only that person you call "mother", can jump straight out of bed,
On one hour of sleep, with a painful pounding head.
Get the kids up, dressed and fed, get them off to school,
Put in eight more hours, until her work day is through.

Only a special lady called "mother", can play and master both roles,
Give it all that she has in her, plus all of her heart and soul.
Only a" mother" each day of her life, can juggle those two jobs,
Then come straight home from work, do laundry, cook and mop.

Only a caring "mother", sits up until you get home,
No matter what age you are, twelve, fifteen or if you think you're grown.
Only a loving "mother", can instantly heal a child's boo-boo,
With very little effort, a band- aid, hug and "I love you".

Only a real "mother", can mend the pains of puppy love,
And think no guy that's breathing, is ever worthy of.
Her little girl that's so innocent, her child that's so naive,
Only a "mother's" love begins, the moment you're conceived.

Only a loving "mother", will always care and love you,
No matter the choices you make or the wrong that you may do.
Only that woman you call "mother", would give her very own life,
Never ponder her decision, never think about it twice.

Only a true "mother", will always be there till the end,
Your" mother" is your most, devout, loyal, trusted friend.
Only a "mother's" love, outweighs all others, yes everyone's,
Only a "mother's' love, is as close to God's love as it comes.

Spreading Her Wings

Sometimes I think you can hardly wait, to leave this place called home,
You feel the urge to spread your wings, go tackle life alone.
I know that I will be so sad, the day you decide to go,
But while you're still here, there are a few things you need to know.

Being all "grown up" now, consist of several different things,
There's lots of good and lots of bad and too much in between.
Responsibility can be a challenging, major factor in your world,
You're now a grown up lady, gone are the days of that little girl.

There's car insurance, car payments, rent and electricity,
Things you're not accustom to paying for, trust me one day you will see.
There's cable and internet and all your food that I now buy,
You'll wonder how I did it, don't feel bad, so have I.

There are cell phone bills, renters insurance, things you don't know about,
Go check out my check book, if ever you're in doubt.
Medical and life insurance, now they never cross your mind,
But one day soon you'll face all of this, it's just a matter of time.

It's time you made your own decisions, live life without my rules,
My main concern is you'll continue, to keep the morals that I taught you.
You'll no longer have a curfew and no longer live with me,
When the newness of independence wears off, things will change, you'll see.

It's not just fun and thrills, being out there on your own,
With nobody to answer to or to tell you right from wrong.
No one to bail you out, when the going gets too tough,
But my home is always open, when grown up life becomes too much.

As Long As I Live

As long as I live you won't be forgotten, even if I die today,
As long as I live, you'll be loved even past the grave.
As long as I live, your memory will stay alive,
That's one thing you can bank on, until the day I die.

As long as I live, I'll be your trusted friend,
That you can count on, since my love has no end.
As long as I live, I'll stand right by your side,
My loyalty for you, in no way will I ever deny.

As long as I live, I'll always protect you,
No matter where you go, no matter what you do.
As long as I live, you'll have a place to stay,
That remains true, even when God calls me away.

As long as I live, you'll always have a home,
As long as I live, you'll never walk alone.
As long as I live, you'll always have a mother,
And as long as I live, you're priority above all others.

I Keep It All Inside

I keep it all inside, I've always been that way,
I'm sure that I'll remain like this, until my dying days.
I don't like to bother others, really what's the need,
They have enough to deal with, other than to worry about me.

I keep it all inside, there's no point in letting it out,
Especially when many others are much worse off no doubt.
I keep it all inside, because people think I'm so strong,
Little do they realize, some days I'm barely holding on.

I keep it all inside, I hide my emotions so very well,
When I'm depressed, sad, or happy, to others it's hard to tell.
I keep it all well hidden, in this tender heart of mine,
I'm not one to complain, share my pain, or whine.

I keep it all inside, one day I'm bound to explode,
When it all comes crashing down and I take the time to unload.
Yes I keep things deep inside, I'm too old now to change,
If I acted like some others, y'all wouldn't look at me the same.

A Mother's Love

You taught us how to pray at night, taught us right from wrong.
You taught us to believe in God, you gave us a loving home.
You taught us to always do our best, no matter what others do.
And to do unto others, as you'd have them do unto you.

You said, "You reap whatever you sow, be careful the steps you take,
Because the path you choose has a way of coming home to you someday".
You said "It's best to give than to receive and always help the weak,
 To live our lives, humble, mild mannered and meek. "

A mother's love is next to God's, that's what I've always heard,
If I searched the world over, I'd find no truer words.
I've never seen you lose your temper or take God's name in vain,
Never heard you curse at others or play the cheaters game.

I've never known you to tell a lie, you're trustworthy till the end,
You've never worn a proud look or back-stabbed a friend.
I could write for eternity and never say quiet enough,
About the mother that taught us, about unconditional love.

In my eyes you're picture perfect and that you can believe,
And anyone who knows you, I'm sure they all would agree.
If I live to be one hundred, I'll always give God thanks,
For blessing me with a mother that made me who I am today.

Words of a Fireman

I'll be back soon, as he tightly hugs his wife,
This is my calling, to save someone's life.
I need you to gear up, don't forget your SCBA,
Address is 6455, down on Chadwick Lane.

The winds picking up, that's not a good sign,
Let's get this truck rolling, while there's still time.
Run all the stop signs, all the stop lights too,
Seconds makes the biggest difference, in all that you do.

The Incident Commander, is in charge of this scene,
The roofs collapsing, God help us with this thing.
The fires really blazing, it's headed for the attic,
We need to contain this, before there's a panic.

It's a twenty floor building, ten are already down,
There's a little girl crying, she has to be found.
There's a fireman down, get him on a stretcher,
You're welcome Sir, it's an honor and a pleasure.

Call my wife, tell her I love her and it's gonna be okay,
She knows I'll be going, to a much better place.
Tell the kids, daddy loves them, each and every night,
And to take good care of mommy, till we meet on the other side.

Kids

Kids can do the funniest things, then act like they're so grown up,
This doesn't start later in life, they're in diapers and holding a sippy cup.
Everything they see amazes them, like bright lights, colors and noise,
Balls, dolls, trains, trucks, in fact any kind of toy.

When they start crawling, they get into everything,
Climbing on chairs and tables, they rarely stay in their swings.
Next you try to figure out, their gibber-jabber baby talk,
They think they've hit the big time, when they began to walk.

You teach them to finger paint and when coloring to stay in the lines,
How to tie their shoes with an actual string, not the Velcro kind.
You are ever so very careful, when teaching them to ride a bike,
You go through several types of food, to find out what they like.

Next there are swimming lessons, that put your patience to a test,
Ask any kid if they can swim and their answer is always yes.
Age doesn't matter, you'll always get the same reply,
Whether they are one or two, three or four or especially at age five.

When they start kindergarten, by now they should know how to act,
They learn to write their name, their ABC's and a little math.
When they finally get to high school, by then they know it ALL,
They think they magically knew everything and the part you played was so small.

9-11-2001

Who in America could ever forget, that sad September day,
When so many lives were lost, yet so many others were saved?
343 Firemen died, giving it their very all,
I bet there's not one true American, that really can't recall.

About 3000 horrible deaths, on that Tuesday morn,
Killing fathers, mothers, daughters, sons and the unborn.
Approximately 3000 later died, from exposure to dust from the site.
All because of terrorist, what a senseless, useless fight.

Sadly terrorist are raised, only to kill and fight,
It's an honor to them all, to take innocent lives.
They will kill their very own, in a blink of an eye,
Never feel one bit of remorse, walk away all smiles.

When the 4 planes went down, 19 hijackers were on board,
They knew they would die too, death to them is a glorifying reward.
Can you even imagine, the amount of blood shed that day,
In less than 20 minutes, the World Trade Center was wiped away?

American Airlines flight 77 crashed the Pentagon outside of DC,
Terrifying, screaming bodies, engulfed the Land of the Free.
United Airlines flight 93, crashed in a field in PA,
To all of the survivors, American's hearts go out to you each day.

Can your mind comprehend, having to make that final call,
To your wife, son, or daughter, saying "daddy loves you all?"
Or calling your husband, your dear mother, or your dad,
As you're blowing kisses through the phone, trying not to sound so sad.

Or saying, "Be good for mommy, you'll always be daddy's girl".
Or telling your mother, "You're the greatest mom in the world".
Trying to hold back your tears, trying to be so brave and strong,
Knowing your life is over, when you hang up the phone.

Things That Shrink Your Clothes

I just discovered several things, that will surely shrink your clothes,
Chocolate cake, hot fudge sundaes, are among a list of those.
Cheese-baked casseroles, those delicious homemade fries,
Cheesecake, cookies and that American apple pie.

Potatoes with a lot of butter and also mac and cheese,
I can't think of anyone, that doesn't like any of these.
Cream-based soups and biscuits made with buttermilk,
Pecan pie, sausage and bacon, yes I love all of this.

Hot dogs, cheeseburgers, deep-dish pizzas too,
Chicken fried steak with gravy and that mouthwatering fondue.
Whole milk, too much beer, cokes and sweet ice tea,
That oh so good movie popcorn, carries 1200 calories.

Any type of toaster pastries, even though they are easy to fix,
Eating too many of these, always shows up on your hips.
Pancakes, French toast, maple syrup and ice cream,
Krispy Kreme donuts, they have a tendency to split your seams.

Fried chops, fried chicken, ribs and potato chips,
All of these shrink your clothes, the moment they touch your lips.
You could try to avoid these foods and prove you're really strong,
Or tell folks the problem is, your clothes stayed in the dryer too long.

Innocence

The innocence of a baby or the innocence of a kid,
Before they grow up and regret, so many things that they once did.
The innocence of that four year old, still believing in ole Saint Nick,
The Easter bunny, the tooth fairy, that ended all too quick.

The innocence of a six year old boy, when he goes to the candy store,
Just to spend his money, on that six year old girl next door.
The innocence of any child, before they learn to hate,
The innocence of that little girl, the day that she turns eight.

The innocence of that ten year old, when she thinks he's the one,
Little does she know at this age, her life's all about having fun.
The innocence of that thirteen year old, with her heart throbbing crush,
But in reality all along, it was only puppy love.

The innocence of a teenage girl, stuck between a woman and a child,
So many mixed emotions, running through her squeaky clean mind.
Actually the innocence of any child, since all humans they easily trust,
Adults need to be more like them and they need to be a lot less like us.

How To Begin Your day

First start with a good cup of coffee, Folgers or Maxwell House,
Get up before all others, when everything is quiet as a mouse.
Have some time for yourself, before your daily rush begins,
Keep a good attitude, find that inner peace within.

Read a scripture from the Bible, like the Book of Proverbs,
Live by what you read, yes each and every word.
Turn on your television and catch the morning news,
Then watch that beautiful sun rise, then glimpse the morning dew.

Go to work real early and give it all you've got,
Keep a positive perspective, joke and laugh a lot.
Keep your heart full of compassion, try to always wear a smile,
Live life for the moment, things you only capture once in a while.

Remember to stay calm, don't let others spoil your day,
Watch your words and actions, at school, at work or at play.
All of the above I've written, is a good way to begin your day,
And if you try it sometime, you just might like it this way.

The Man In The Mirror

When you think you've done a great job, with that word we all call life,
And you seek the approval, from your husband or your wife.
Your boss pats you on the back and you display plaques that you've won,
Just look into the mirror and see what that man thinks you've done.

When your friends ring out praises, of the kind of man you are,
And no matter where you go, you're treated like a super star.
You're respected in your community, amid the upper class,
But does that man in the mirror agree, when you look into that glass.

When your day comes to an end and you're home with family,
Do you feel as if today, you've been all that you could be?
Would the man in the mirror, be proud of the things you did today,
Or can you look him in the eye, pleased with what others think and say?

The man staring in the mirror is more than a picture of you,
He's also your conscience and sees everything that you do.
So make sure you make him proud, no matter what others believe,
Cause he's the one that really knows you, the one you can't deceive.

Loneliness

Do you ever feel alone or feel like no one cares,
And when you're feeling down, seems no one is ever there?
Do you feel betrayed by love ones, that you dearly love so,
You don't know where to turn, there's really nowhere to go?

Do you often feel let down, by folks that claim to be your friend,
Still you give them many chances, time and time again?
Do you ever feel like loneliness, has totally consumed your life,
And you and you alone, deals with your troubles and your strife?

Do you feel you'd be a burden, if others knew how you feel,
Or if they wouldn't understand or think it's no big deal?
Do you consider yourself a loner, feel as if you don't fit in,
And no matter what you do, someone's eager to condemn?

Everybody needs somebody, that's just how this life is,
The impact of a warm embrace, works magic with any of this.
Just to know that someone cares, isn't such a demanding request,
Take the time to help someone, with this word called loneliness.

If Tomorrow Starts Without Me

If tomorrow starts without me, I'd like for you to know,
To me you were everything, I hope to you that it showed.
You were the air in my lungs, the beat within my heart,
The reason I kept on going, even when I didn't want to start.

I've always mentioned your name, in every prayer I've ever prayed,
You're the reason I went to work, day after day, after day.
You totally occupied my thoughts, yes you're always on my mind,
Constantly keeping tabs on you, to make sure you were all right.

You've always been my sunshine, even when skies were dark and grey,
The years we've spent together, nobody can take away.
You have always needed me and I've always needed you too,
There's not much in this world, that I wouldn't have done for you.

You've made me a better person, with a heart that's tender and true,
Whatever good I've done in this life, I did it all just for you.
So if tomorrow starts without me and I'm not there to see,
Remember if you have ever been loved, you were surely loved by me.

You Think You Have It Bad

I ride the roads a lot, you'd be amazed at the things I see,
So sit back and brace yourself, these things you won't believe.
Oh I wish I hadn't seen them, it made me thankful but so sad,
So just reread this poem, when you think you have it so bad.

I saw a man at an apartment, digging a four foot ditch,
At least ten feet long, through dirt hard as a brick.
The sad part of this scenario, he had one arm and one hand,
His disabilities didn't stop him, he's a one of a kind man.

I also witnessed a lady, sitting cross legged on her lawn,
Cutting her grass with scissors, since a mower she didn't own.
My heart melted like butter, as I hurried on my way,
Asking God to help her, was the prayer that day I prayed.

As recently as this week, I saw something I'm compelled to share,
A woman was pushing her mower, from an electric wheelchair.
I thought why don't someone, have compassion and do this task,
Had I not been working, I would have gladly cut her grass.

Someone is always in much worse shape, than you will ever be,
These unimaginable, heart-wrenching things, so many days I often see.
So when you start complaining and think you have it so bad,
Thank your lucky stars, you haven't seen the things I have.

When Everything Is Gone

It seems like anything goes, once everything to you is gone,
You often question God, wondering what you did so wrong.
Some opt to hit the bottle and never quite put it down,
Some turn to addictive drugs, thinking hope just can't be found.

Or maybe there was an accident, on highway 903,
You saw it on the news, then your telephone starts to ring.
As she lays there dying, you feel helpless and so alone,
She was your only child, to you everything is now gone.

He packs all of his belongings, it cuts you to the core,
All you see is tail lights and hear the slamming of a door.
You blaming him for everything, of course he blames you too,
There's three sides to every story, yours, his and the cold hard truth.

You've loved her most of your life, well over sixty years,
You're standing by her bedside, her time on earth is drawing near.
You fall down upon your knees, begging God not to call her home,
To you your life is now nothing, since your everything is now gone.

No matter what cards you're dealt, cautiously play each hand,
Even when life seems unbearable and it's so hard to understand.
Just keep your eyes on Jesus, for with Him you can't go wrong,
Sadly sometimes anything goes, when everything to you is gone.

My Favorite Memories

Having the very best childhood and great parents to boot,
Me in my Easter clothes, my brothers in their little suits.
Swimming lessons my grandmother, took us to everyday,
She'd sit in that hot car, as we swam, dived and played.
My grandmother curling my hair, putting me in a dress,
Her cooking was incredible, her love was the very best.
Trying to play softball, we broke several bones,
It didn't take long to realize, a stage is where we belonged.
Memories of me as a child, with a guitar in my hand,
Trying to be like my dad, playing and singing in a band.
Remembering my piano teacher, she was at least ninety years old,
She had the eyes of an eagle, she was fearless, talented and bold.
Playing in the school band, at Elm City High,
Guitar, piano, trumpet and French horn to my surprise.
Turning sixteen in the hospital, on a Wednesday in the middle of May,
Pneumonia from going barefooted, just one night and then one day.
Finishing high school, going straight to work and such,
Wanting to be independent, couldn't wait to grow up.
Moving to Nashville Tennessee at the age of twenty-three,
Playing the Grand Ole Opry, my most pleasurable memory.
My precious niece being born, in August of seventy-nine,
Instantly she stole my heart, I soon considered her mine.

The birth of my nephew, a head full of curly hair,
His grandparents and mother spoiling him, he had the best of care.
Playing music in all of the churches, in our family gospel band,
My dad preaching to the children, every woman and every man.
Going to a little white church, at least three times a week,
Learning about the Bible, calling God's name upon my knees.
We discovered we could make money, if we took it on the road,
Booking show dates in the beginning, so little did we know.
Practicing in my daddy's barn, so we could compete with the rest,
Drilling it into our heads, nobody wants to be second best.
Playing thirty years every weekend and during the weekdays too,
A tight fit musical family, doing what we loved to do.
Then experiencing motherhood, at the age of thirty-nine,
I wasn't sure if I could do that, but it all turned out just fine.
Memories of mama's cooking, her baking the best cakes and pies,
I'd give everything that I own, to have a slice of hers tonight.
The very best chicken pastry, homemade biscuits out of this world,
The morals that she instilled into, her boys and her girl.
These are some of my favorite memories, way too many to list them all,
These easily come to mind, each time I stop to recall.
Each special memory that I have, fills my heart with glee,
I have been so very blessed, to have such wonderful memories.

Somewhere Tonight

Somewhere tonight, a mother's fighting for her life,
Somewhere across town, a young girl's walking down the aisle.
Somewhere tonight, an old man is living alone,
Somewhere else in the world, God is calling someone home.

Somewhere tonight, a man is sleeping in the park,
Somewhere down the road, a child is afraid of the dark.
Somewhere tonight, a house is being robbed,
Unfortunately just about anywhere, someone just lost their job.

Somewhere tonight, a teenager packs and runs away,
Somewhere in a nursing home, sits a mother old and grey.
Somewhere tonight, someone took their own life,
Somewhere at a party, someone fell in love at first sight.

Somewhere tonight, a dad just had a stroke,
Somewhere in a neighborhood, a house went up in smoke.
Somewhere tonight, a heart is breaking right into,
And somewhere at this moment, someone is being untrue.

Somewhere tonight, 911 is being called,
Somewhere tonight, a soldier gives his all.
Somewhere tonight, people are praying for inner peace,
And someone every night, prays to God down on their knees.

Love

Love doesn't come with instructions, you kinda roll with the flow,
Love isn't always prepared, for something different down the road.
Love's the very last thing, that will give up and walk away,
Love has a way of working things out and forever does it stay.

Love is full of kindness, putting others before yourself,
Love is those sacred vows and no matter what they're upheld.
Love is full of honesty, there just isn't room for any lies,
Love is also comforting, when someone starts to cry.

Love is full of patience, keeping a firm grip on your tongue,
Love is truly caring, for the older folks and the young.
Love is also forgiveness, no matter what they've done,
Love is letting them know, they are your number one.

Love is always present, when a mother is giving birth,
Love is total respect, with yes ma'am and no sirs.
Love is filled with compassion, for the homeless on the streets,
Love is spreading hope and cheer, to everyone that you meet.

Love always steps up to the plate and going that extra mile,
Love is turning someone's frown, into an instant smile.
Love is the strongest word, that there has ever been,
Search your heart cause love can be found, hidden down deep within.

Erasers

Have you wished you could erase something from your past?
Maybe a relationship that you once wished would last,
Or erase that terrible argument, even though you won,
And start back at the point, to where it all begun.

Perhaps erase a million, of those selfish, careless, thoughts,
Or erase the times you actually, quarreled, bickered and fought?
Maybe erase that crush that secretly you still have today,
And hope that one day soon, those feelings will go away.

Maybe erase those times, you talked back to your mom,
Even erase that date that took you to the senior prom.
Erase all those many times, you were the bully at your school,
The days you thought you were all that and thought you were so cool.

Erase every single lie, that you have ever told,
And all of those moments, when your temper took control.
Perhaps you'd like to erase that day, when you lost a very good job,
The heartless times you were cruel, arrogant or a snob?

Do you desire to erase the nights that you wasted in some old bar,
Drinking way to many, while breaking several hearts?
The night that your drunk driving claimed an innocent life,
Twenty years in prison, living with it day and night.

We have all been there, bad choices we chose to make,
Things we did in life, we wish we could magically erase.
You need to live in the present, forget past mistakes you've made,
The things you did forever ago, just simply can't be erased.

But I Did It

Sometimes I often wondered, how I could pay a certain bill,
And everything I faced in life, always seemed to be uphill.
Many times I've questioned God, although I know it's wrong,
Yet every day I still thank Him for keeping me holding on.

Many years have now gone by, with me always playing both roles,
Being both mom and dad, can easily take its toll.
There have been many trying days, I wondered what I should do,
Many times I cried out to God, He would always get me through.

For nineteen long years now, I've prayed both day and night,
That no matter what I was up against, my kid would turn out right.
That she would have a good heart and full of compassion too,
Strive to make wise decisions and be nobody's fool.

I've prayed for many others, also prayed for my family,
And to keep me together, since they all needed me.
I've driven an old Toyota, for years to me it seems,
But it still gets me where I need to go, from point A to point B.

In some of my weakest moments, I often felt like giving up,
I hold onto precious memories, I've known love, pain and hurt.
Some decisions I've made were foolish, some crazy I must admit,
But with God holding my hand, I made it through all of this.

I did all of this and more, sometimes I wondered how,
Thanks to my God above, things are so much better now.
God and I just somehow, seem to make the perfect team,
I did it with God's help, He brought out the best in me.

The Hardest Words To Say

Sometimes just saying "hello", can be so hard to do,
Especially if you're shy and words you speak are few.
Also saying "I love you", for the very first time,
Even if those three words were buried in the back of your mind.

Saying "I've found another, after all the years I held onto us
Because one too many times, you betrayed my trust".
Saying "I want a divorce, even though I love you still,
Some things never change, at times I think I always will."

Saying "my time on earth is coming to an end,
I've been a mother, a daughter, a wife, I've also been a caring friend."
Saying "I need help," when you don't know what to do,
Saying "I'm truly sorry for all that I've put you through."

Saying "I was wrong again" and "yes all along you've been right",
Or "will you marry me and love me the rest of your life?"
Saying "I haven't been honest, I've told too many lies",
"You're better off without me" as you finally lost all pride.

Saying that sad, final "goodbye", for the very last time,
Saying "after some time has passed, go on with your life".
The hardest words to say, often changes the rest of our lives,
But when all is said and done, things have a way of turning out alright.

Things I Miss The Most

That sweet sea foam candy, that my mother use to make,
My grandmother's eight layered, homemade chocolate cake.
My daddy many years ago, riding me on his back,
Now that I've grown up, I miss those wonderful times like that.

My little girl when she was naive, believing in that man in red and white,
My beloved toy poodle, my constant shadow day and night.
The carefree days before my niece, decided to walk down the aisle,
Those days my three year old, filled me with laughter, hugs and smiles.

My dear sweet grandmother, oh how that lady could cook,
Daddy planting my trees and every shrub and every rose bush.
I surely miss the days, that I actually grew up on a stage,
Of all of my fondest memories, those to me were my greatest days.

Those days forever ago, when I didn't have any bills,
When my five year old played dress-up, in my old clothes and heels.
The golden days of high school, me playing in the marching band,
The days of always having, plenty of extra cash on hand.

I miss those days of driving, that shiny new sports car,
And the days of barning tobacco, even though the work was hard.
I miss the days when my mother, was the center of family events,
Don't we all miss those days, when we didn't have to pay rent?

Everything I miss as an adult, I took for granted as a kid,
But if I could do things over, I'd appreciate childhood more than I did.
I surely have pleasant memories, growing up on the East Coast,
All of the above and so much more, are things I miss the most.

Old Friends

Old friends know so much about you, the good, not so good and the bad,
They keep lifelong secrets, of all the crazy times you once had.
Some are closer than a sister and stick closer than a twin,
Some you'll forever make memories with, time and time again.

Old friends come to your rescue, no matter the time of night,
To comfort and assure you, that everything's gonna be alright.
If you have a flat, twenty-five miles from home,
Old friends are the first to say, "I'll be there before too long."

When you decided to settle down and it's your wedding day,
Old friends step right up, to help out in anyway.
The birth of your little girl, old friends are at your side,
Telling you, you can do this, wiping tears as you cry.

When your grandmother's dying, old friends know what to do,
You support each other, since they called her grandma too.
No matter the obstacles, you're faced with in your life time,
Old friends are the best, I hope everyone has one like mine.

How I was Raised

The most important things I learned in life, wasn't taught in school,
Like kindness, good manners and how to not be another's fool.
To honor your mother and father, always be a good kid,
Keep the vows sacred, like your still married parents did.

At your first argument, don't be so eager to call it quits,
Forgive like you want to be forgiven, just like Jesus did.
Never out grow your raising's, don't walk around looking proud,
Don't disturb the neighbors, keep your voices down.

Go to bed early, greet the dawn with a happy face,
Don't walk through life grumpy, strive to make someone's day.
Get an honest day's pay for working, do your best in all you do,
Smile at people in passing, abide by the golden rule.

Start raising your kids early, don't wait until they turn 16,
Then wonder where you went wrong, because they didn't learn a thing.
You've all so often read, about these great parents of mine,
I'll take the good old fashion raising, any day and any time.

If You Could Rewind Time

What would you do, if you could go back in time,
Would you do things different, most would, so would I?
Would you regret the mistakes, you made along the way,
Or perhaps be content, with who you are today?

Would you listen to your parents more, lived by their rules,
Gone on to finish college and never dropped out of school?
Would you have been more careful, about your choice of friends,
Would you have fell in and out of love, time and time again?

If you could do it over, would you have lit that first cigarette,
Have more money now, instead of paying gambling debts?
Would you have ever stepped into, what became a bar after bar,
Would you have never driven drunk, the night you wrecked your car?

Would you still have your child, the one you never get to see,
Would you have signed away your rights, when she was barely three?
How about those drugs, would you have ever tried them out,
Would you now believe in God, without a shadow of a doubt?

Would you have used bad language, in front of your little kids,
Then ten years down the road, wonder why they turned out like they did?
Would you be ever so pleased, with the choices you made in life,
Or would you do things differently, if you could just rewind time?

Nothing Last Forever

That 1998 Toyota, with over five hundred thousand miles,
Nothing last forever but in it I still ride.
This home we live in, could use some major repairs,
Another coat of paint would be good and a new set of stairs.

The computer we're on, every night and every day,
Sooner or later, it will have to be replaced.
Those designer jeans many years ago, once fit you to a "T",
Wearing them now is a hassle, still into them you try to squeeze.

That sports car was once so cool, shiny, bright and new,
Now the color has faded and it needs more tires too.
That mattress you sleep on, night after night,
You now need a new one, because it sags on one side.

The washer and dryer, once was top of the line,
Now it dances and wobbles, there's your sign.
Your skin was so long ago, smooth and wrinkle free,
Nothing last forever, I'm sure we will all agree.

What is a Song

A song is a mixture of words, often both good and bad,
It can put you on the highest high, it can make you ever so sad.
A song can make you get up and dance, make you long for another,
It can also make you reminisce, about your long ago ex- lover.

A song can make you feel the rhythm, make you hum the tune,
Make your drive seem so much shorter, take away all of your gloom.
Songs come in all kinds of flavors, such as ballads, rap and pop,
Country, gospel, blue grass and also jazz and rock.

The band makes the singer, the singer makes the song,
The song can soothe your mind, all night and all day long.
A song is actually a poem written, with music added in,
Drums, bass, guitars and keyboards, makes your poetic blend.

What would life be without music or a song without a voice,
A singer without a song, not much of a reason to rejoice?
So when you're counting your blessings, count one for music,
If you have a talent to sing, play or write, use it so you won't lose it.

The Life of a Musician

I learned how to play several instruments, when I was very young,
Trumpet, piano, guitar, bass, organ and drums.
A musician seems to focus on just one thing in life,
How they sounded on stage, making sure the words came out right.

The drummer is ALWAYS late, when it's time to set up,
And always the very last, to get his drums into the truck.
The keyboard player seems, to always have to sing,
All parts of the harmony and sometimes the lead.

Let's take that guitar player, he just has to be heard,
Sometimes over-riding the singers, every little word.
The bass man goes BOMP BOMP, all through the night,
The rest of the bands praying, he hits each note perfectly right.

The steel guitar man's job is to make that Emmons cry,
Make it sound like a freight train, rolling in the night.
The rhythm player seems to think he knows it all,
Standing dead center with his Martin, smiling proud and tall.

We don't invest in cheap cords either, they have to be the best,
Microphones like Sennheiser and Shure will surely pass our test.
We may live in a three room shack or drive a beat up car,
But when we hit the stage, look at the price of that guitar.

In a musician's eyes, their instruments must always shine,
They have to be name brand, have to be top of the line.
Emmons, Roland's, Peavey, Pearls and Fenders too,
If you show up with another brand, we won't stand on a stage with you.

If Everyone Could Be Like You

If every breathing soul in this world could be exactly like you,
Would that be a good thing, would you need to change a thing or two?
Would your attitude need adjusting, would your language stay the same,
Or when you looked into the mirror, would you bow your head in shame?

Would you complain just to be complaining, and still continue to grumble?
Would your words be a little kinder and your heart a lot more humble?
Would you remain ill and moody or be kinda laid back mellow?
Would you do a whole lot more daily, to help the other fellow?

Would you attend church more often, or trot off to another bar?
Would you be nicer to your neighbor, or do you even know who they are?
Would you be proud of who you are and proud of everything you do?
How would the whole world be, if everyone was exactly like you?

Social Services

It's a good thing I'm not a Social Worker, the system would go broke,
If anyone came in my office, needing food, shelter or clothes.
Knowing me I'd finagle the forms they just filled out,
Just so that they could qualify without a single doubt.

Example a single moms income is only twelve hundred bucks,
She has three kids to care for, no child support and down on her luck.
There's rent and those school supplies and that high electricity,
I'd say that she needs help, any caring heart would agree.

There will always be doctor and dentist bills, even if you rarely go,
Sooner or later we all know, you're gonna need one of those.
According to Medicaid policies, she happens to be too rich,
I'll tell you one thing folks, I don't agree with any of this.

Especially when a child's involved, she would leave with all I could give,
And never again in their life would this needy moment be relived.
For God sake don't let it be Christmas, we'd have to close the doors,
But by then I would have given out, all we had and more.

Then in the month of January when they begin to audit the books,
You'd see me in the unemployed line, another job I'd have to look.
So it's best I stay right where I am and travel from home to home,
At least it's job security, home health is where I belong.

I Think I've Lost My Mind

I came in here looking for something, wonder what it could be,
Was I looking for my glasses or looking for my keys?
The baby needs changing, I need a diaper and some wipes,
Or does she need a bottle, I think I'm losing my mind?

I went into the kitchen to make me a glass of tea,
But I forgot what I wanted, Lord have mercy on me.
I went to the bathroom, to run water into the tub,
It was already half full, with a lot of bubbles and suds.

Then I went to the couch, to take a much needed nap,
However when I woke up, there was coffee in my lap.
I went outside today, with cutting grass on my mind,
I have no clue who mowed the lawn but it sure looked mighty fine.

I went to the closet, to get out a pair of shoes,
I heard someone knocking but I couldn't imagine who.
I went to the door, told the little boy to get inside,
I don't even have a son, I've finally lost my mind.

Little Eyes, Little Ears

When a child enters your life, you're the first face that they see,
From their very first smile and especially when they learn to speak.
Little eyes and little ears, have them both set straight on you,
So be careful what you say, be careful in all that you do.

If you use bad language, don't be shocked when they do too,
Cause a child's merely a miniature carbon copy of you.
When they see the things you do, make sure those things are good,
Kids need a great example so they will turn out like they should.

It would be wise to watch your actions because little eyes always see,
Everything you don't want them to and that you can believe.
A child lives what they learn at home, this statement is so true,
Little eyes and little ears, grow up to be just like you.

Innocent Minds

What's in the mind of a newborn when the first face she sees is you,
I wonder if in her little thoughts, she's possibly wondering too?
That three year old playing dress-up, I wonder what's on her mind,
Is she thinking perhaps one day, of being a fashion model of some kind?

What does a four year old think, when she's playing with her dolls,
Wonder if she's pretending to be a mom, even though she's still so small?
Through the mind of a little boy playing with his GI Joe's,
Will he someday join the military, Heaven only knows?

That five year old that took ballet, is her dream to someday dance,
And that six year old that's amazed by being a cop if given the chance?
In the mind of a seven year old, when the firemen visit his school,
Will that impact his decision to put out fires, I really wish we knew?

Then you have that ten year old, that wants to cook and clean all day,
She may be the next Paula Deen, if things turn out her way.
So what do little minds think, what goes through an innocent head?
When I was younger I wanted to be a musician/writer, so my parents said.

Being An Orphan

Do you know what it's like to lose both mom and dad,
To be truly alone in a world that's so scary and sad?
All you have is precious memories, that will one day fade away,
Especially if your parents died when you were very young in age.

Being an orphan affects you, in at least four different ways,
Mentally, physically, emotionally and if you'll be successful one day.
All orphans share similar situations, feeling alone and with trust issues,
Some become prostitutes, criminals and even sexually abused.

They are without a parent or someone, that really cares about their life,
No mentor to console in and no one always by their side.
Every child needs stability and love shown in every way,
Encouragement and someone to lean on, each and every day.

The majority of all orphans feel the very same way,
Insecure with themselves, reliving that nightmare day after day.
Orphans can have the chance to actually live like a normal child,
So adopt and reap the rewards of going that extra mile.

Wonderful Lady and Nurse

My mind goes back to when I first met you, so many years ago,
We met at a patients house, in less than five minutes your character showed.
I knew at that very moment, you'd be a great asset,
With your compassion for the human race, you'd soon be one of the best.

You've always been so gentle and caring for other's needs,
No matter what you ask for, your request always starts with please.
You never fail to say "thank you" if someone does you a favor,
You give the credit to others as if they were truly your life saver.

Even when you have bad days, like we all so often do,
You're still as nice as you can be, your good heart still shines through.
You're honest and reliable, a hard worker to say the least,
When others can't see eye to eye, it's you that unites the peace.

Whether it's in the office or in the field, you really know your stuff,
There are so many peers of yours that wish they knew half as much.
Your strong faith in God and your heart-warming personality,
Is what all others admire in you and what we all should strive to be.

Teachers

In these days and times the teachers have it tough in every way,
From the politics of how they can teach, down to their amount of pay.
They work way too many hours, on way too little sleep,
A mentor and a counselor, grading homework and they also teach.

Teachers are disrespected, by at least 70% of all the kids,
All because they're not allowed to teach like they once did.
Now the kids are so out of control and think that schools a joke,
Had they been raised like I was raised, they would listen when teachers spoke.

Back in my younger years, there were very few problems at school,
Because parents trained their kids at home to do what they were told to do.
You never heard of shootings, gangs or using a knife,
God forbid if you talked back, you had better thought twice.

That alone got yourself a whooping, that to this day you still remember,
Heaven help you when you got home, it was worse than no Santa in December.
Parents always took the time to mold and raise their own kids,
And the teacher was always right, no matter what you did.

We didn't start any trouble, no kind of bullying was allowed,
Nobody thought they were cooler, everyone belonged to the same crowd.
No lying and no stealing, you went to school to learn,
We didn't jump in front of others, you knew to wait your turn.

My hats off to anyone, who tries to teach today,
With these types of children, God bless teachers is all I can say.
We started school with The Pledge of Allegiance and then we always prayed,
When they took God and discipline out of schools, look how kids turn out today.

Watching My Mother

She's always sitting in her recliner, watching people walking by,
She mostly stays in a good mood but sometimes she starts to cry.
That's when this loving heart of mine instantly melts like butter,
The things I see would shock you, while I'm watching my mother.

She looks at all the pictures but can't recall many names,
But she will stare at them forever as my eyes fill up with pain.
She glances at the TV but don't know what's going on,
But if she hears a hymn, she has no problem singing along.

She never asks for anything and everything is fine with her,
However she does seem content, in her own sweet little world.
It amazes me the things she remembers, more so the things she don't,
Simple things amuse her so little does she ever want.

Most days she don't know my name, so I stopped asking a while ago,
But she smiles and says "I love you", that's all I need to know.
She loves her stuffed dog named Buster, Dumbo the elephant too,
Would others think I'm coping well, if they spent a day in my shoes?

Defense Lawyers

How does a lawyer defend a man that rapes a five year old child,
Or a man that killed his wife, with that smirky non-caring smile?
How could he defend a woman that sold her kid for drugs,
Then try to convince the jury, her child she really loved?

How does a lawyer defend a twenty year old that shot and killed his mother,
And also killed his dad and sister and once his so close twin brother?
How do they defend a woman, that drowned all five of her kids,
I wonder do they sleep well at night, like they all once did?

How can you defend someone, you know is as guilty as sin,
Or come up with all kinds of excuses of why they did what they did?
I wonder if defense lawyers would want a criminals life spared,
If these things happened to their family ,they'd opt for the electric chair?

Your Job

Do you really like your job, had you rather be at another place?
Is it merely a source of income, another dreaded day to face?
Do you enjoy getting out of bed, seeing what the new day will bring,
Or do you wake up complaining, among many other things?

Do you wish you were wealthy and didn't punch a clock,
Or long for retirement day, oh how you easily forgot?
That those unemployed people, would trade places with you so fast,
Thanking God they had a job, no matter how long it would last.

How many really enjoy, the title that they're accustomed to?
Would you change it in a flash, if it was up to you?
Do you like your employer or is it just a place to be,
At least five days a week, with those benefits that you need?

Even when I'm tired, I try to give it my very best,
And always be ever so thankful and remember how I'm so blessed.
I love this job I have that I can honestly say,
It's challenging yet rewarding, I wish everyone could feel this way.

Teenagers

I'll never understand them, no matter what age they may be,
From thirteen years old to twenty, they think they know everything.
They act as if adults are naive and they don't even have a clue,
They think we didn't do some of the things that they now try to do.

They all think they are so slick and all parents are totally dumb,
All adults were just born old, never once were they ever young.
They know all of life's answers, the adults don't know a thing,
If I make it through her teenage years, it will be a shock to me.

They can instantly cop an attitude over the least important things,
They act like it's a true crisis or so to them it seems.
They have at least five BFF's, how can that possibly be true?
When I grew up you had one best friend, all others were just friends to you.

Times sure have changed a lot and may I add it's for the worse,
Nowadays kids go to jail, lie, steal, fight, kill and curse.
Had I had been any of the above, I wouldn't have been here to write,
My mother knew how to get her point across and she was always right.

The good thing is she's almost grown and I'm now in the short rows,
God only knows how I raised her, since not one thing did I know.
Soon she'll leave for college and then I'll be all alone,
After she's gone it will amaze me, how much she'll think I've grown.

Only In The South

Only in the south, do you always have two seasons,
In the very same week, you go from scorching hot to freezing.
You're seeing the 30's or lower at night and 70's during the day,
It makes you wonder if the North ever has it that way.

Down in the south we just don't get a lot of snow,
But when we do, we make sure that everyone knows.
We rush to make snow-cream before it melts away,
Its ice-cream from Heaven, what a wonderful fun-filled day.

Sometimes we make a snowman, if we get enough snow,
We use charcoal for his eyes and a carrot for his nose.
We use any kind of hat to cover his bald head,
We play and play in the snow until we freeze to death.

Others might laugh at us and think we've lost our minds,
But snow to us is a luxury and in the south it's so hard to find.
To put it plain and simple, to us there's nothing any finer,
Than waking up to a blanket of snow, here in North Carolina.

Too Much On One's Heart

Do you have too much on your heart, or way too much on your mind,
Things that just won't disappear, no matter how hard you try?
Is there too much on your shoulders, too many burdens you have to bare,
Way too many problems that you choose with others not to share?

Are you living proof that ulcers don't come from stress alone?
Do you wish you could go to sleep, wake up and all trials would be gone?
Do you wonder if God's testing your patience and your heart,
To help you decide who is a real friend, when your world's falling apart?

Does anyone ever say to you, "hey how are you these days",
Or do they care about themselves and go about their merry way?
Are they too busy with their own life, to place a simple phone call,
A text, a message or an email, something to show they care at all?

You can bet your last dollar if the circumstances were reversed,
You would never hesitate and you would be the very first.
To make them open up and stop holding all the pain in,
Times like these shows the difference between an acquaintance and a friend.

Things That Are Good For My Heart

On the days that my dear mother actually knows me by name,
Days we have sunshine, instead of cold freezing rain.
Days if only a few hours that I totally feel stress free,
The days I have more time to spend on my knees.
The days where laughter outweighs all of the frowns,
Days where nothing at all seems to get me down.
Those days when my job goes really smooth,
Days when people are kinder and not so ill and rude.
Days when I feel surrounded by caring and concerned friends,
Days when I know my friends are real, not the kind that pretend.
Those days when pain and sorrow doesn't dwell in my life,
The days that I can look into a beautiful Carolina blue sky.
Days when I can take the good and bad all in stride,
Days when I actually listen to a friend's good advice.
Those days I can bring a smile to any given face,
The days that I don't feel like there's too much on my plate.
Those days people pitch in and then do their fair part,
Yes days like these are always good for my heart.
Rare days I don't have to ask God, not for one single thing,
Days I feel by far richer than the wealthiest of all Kings.
Those days that I can sleep with nothing at all on my mind,
The days that everyone is always friendly, sweet and kind.

The days I pray for that stranger that I'm sure I'll never meet,
Days I don't see a sign, saying, "will work for food to eat."
Days I miss that someone and out of the blue they call,
Those days when I often stumble, yet I never seem to fall.
Days my friends are healthy and there's not one complaint,
All the days I'm in the prayers of God's warmhearted saints.
The days I weigh the pros and when I weigh the cons,
That's the days that I realize I'm still much better off.
The days that I'm convinced, no matter what I'm not alone,
Days I can live up to the title of me being tough and strong.
Those days when my mother hasn't one tear in her eyes,
Days I have understanding and I'm not asking God why.
The days my child proves to me that she did turn out alright,
The days that I praise God for all of this day and night.
The days I show compassion and I don't ask for anything,
Those days I help another and the pleasure to me that it brings.
The days my families health is improving quite a lot,
Those days I thank God for all of the things I've got.
The days the mail is delivered and no bills came that day,
Days my dad isn't so worried about my mother in anyway.
All the days I get home safely after traveling several miles,
These kind of days are good for my heart, full of love, peace and smiles.

Is Your World Closing In

Have you ever felt as if your whole world was closing in,
And if others cared enough to listen, would you even know where to begin?
Have you ever wished you could go to sleep, with nothing on your mind,
And wake up to a brand new day filled with peace, smiles and sunshine?

Have you ever wished that someone could take your blues away,
And they could somehow put your mind at ease, if only for one day?
Have you ever longed for a vacation even though it's out of reach,
Just to walk on unfamiliar turf and hopefully find some form of peace?

Have you ever sat in a room with so many people around,
Yet still have the feeling of loneliness, sadness and so low down?
Have you ever humbly asked God, "How strong do you think I am,
"You must think I'm as strong as Sampson, I'm trying hard not to let you down?"

Do you ever feel ashamed, when you see others worse off than you,
So you suck the pain in deeper and just ask God to help you get through?
Have you ever felt as if your hearts been in a blender,
Shattered in so many pieces, needing a white flag waving I surrender?

However being so strong for others is how you've always rolled,
Keeping all the pain inside, sooner or later it's gonna take its toll.
Have you ever felt so helpless, still so many others depend on you,
You never really know how strong you are, you just do what you gotta do?

Do You Have A Conscience

Do you have a clear conscience, do you sleep good at night,
Or no matter what you do to others, do you think you're always right?
Do you think about yourself and put others far down the line?
Does it bother you when they're in need or not as long as you're doing fine?

Do you ever think about your life and all the lies you tell each day,
By now you've told so many, it comes natural to you in every way?
Do you often take from others just to fulfill your selfish wants?
I'm not too sure who raised you, but that's not how I was taught.

Do you have folks believing that you're a real good friend,
When in reality you back stab them, time and time again?
Do you ever help a stranger or do you just simply walk on by?
Do you care less if you make a difference, in anybody else's life?

I bet your promises are convincing and your life's a total mess,
And you're a taker not a giver by taking more and giving less.
If asked, "how do you sleep at night", do you reply, "just like a baby",
That's because you have no conscience, is there hope for you, one day maybe?

Do you take advantage of others and feel no sense of remorse,
I'd say you need to enroll in a, "how to treat others course?"
Does it ever cross your mind, that your heart needs to change,
Or are you proud of who you really are, to me that's a crying shame?

Trust

Does anyone really know the actual meaning of the word trust?
If not I'm here to tell you, so sit back and listen up.
It's not just any five letters used to make a complete word,
Other than love it's the best word you've possibly ever heard.

This word is filled with meaning and many emotions too,
Trust is so important in anything that you ever do.
Without trust, any relationship is automatically doomed,
99% chance of not ever retrieving, at least any time soon.

It takes some time to regain trust but can be lost in no time at all,
You rarely completely get it back, you're always up against a wall.
It's not like flipping an hour glass and starting over again,
Or rewinding time back to where it all began.

You just can't take an eraser and wipe the slate clean,
It's not like emptying a tub then refilling it once again.
So if you ever lose it and you're left feeling betrayed,
No matter what the future holds, things won't ever be the same.

It can be shattered oh so quickly and take years to build back up,
So don't ever take for granted, this valuable word called trust.
Unfortunately it's this simple, once it's gone it's usually gone,
So grasp it so tightly so you'll never face life alone.

Memories

I no longer win all your marbles, we never play a broom straw guitar,
We rarely pitch a baseball or play pool and darts.
Tag is now a child's game, we left back in our past,
The many days at the pool, now won't they a blast?

We never play truth or dare, never attempt to climb a tree,
We never try to jump a rope or run from honey bees.
We rarely ride a bike now, cars have taken its place,
We don't dress up for Halloween or wait to see Santa's face.

We no longer look for Easter eggs or what the bunny brought,
Now we are living the life of all that we've been taught.
We don't dive into a pile of leaves or have a snowball fight,
But these are precious memories, stored in my heart and in my mind.

The days and nights of skating rinks no longer cross our minds,
Wouldn't it be so wonderful to be able to step back into time?
When life was never stressful, where there was never pain,
When all we ever worried about was playing another game.

We never try to catch fire flies, never wish upon shooting stars,
But having you as my brother has made me the luckiest by far.
The best days I remember are the days I spent with you,
I hope your life is filled with happiness and may all your dreams come true.

My Wannabe Boss

I have my own WBB, which stands for "wannabe boss",
Some days I don't need her, other days I'd be totally lost.
Especially when my "real" boss decides to fly out to LA,
And she's not at work to defend me, oh how I hate those days.

She's thrilled to tell me what to do, likes to tell me when I'm wrong,
She jumps for joy and full of laughter, harassing me on the phone.
She's also pleased to tell me, my many mistakes on that Ipad,
Or how I don't use it properly, sometimes she just nags and nags.

She tries to give me a hard time, I give it back as good as she sends,
It's all in a day of work and fun, that's how our days start and end.
She can be so super sweet, especially when she needs a favor,
But when it's all said and done, I wouldn't replace or ever trade her.

I call her the "Warden", she swears I'm something else,
And all of her other thoughts, she reluctantly keeps to herself.
Yes we pick on each other but we really have a ball,
Those days I'm about to crumble, she's there to break my fall.

I have to admit in her defense, she's as real as one can be,
She along with many others, makes me glad to be on her team.
We all get along so good and when the day is done,
Our jobs complete even if we're tired, we went down having fun.

Everything Is Temporary

Everything is just temporary, even your days here on earth,
It's decided early on in life at the beginning of your birth.
There's a temporary relationship that leads you to the right one,
Nobody has control of destiny, it's just how things are done.

There are several temporary jobs, until you find the one that's right,
The one you choose to retire from, working long days and longer nights.
There are temporary arguments, you may experience with your spouse,
A temporary apartment, until you buy that perfect house.

There's temporary quarreling between a sister and a brother,
Nobody else could get by with it, no I can't think of another.
There are temporary cars, that helps you to get by,
Then you find the one you longed for and got it when the time was right.

There's a temporary garden, then you gather up your crops,
There's a temporary person, that was once your heart throb.
There's a temporary flower bed, until that first frost hits,
There's temporary weather that forecasters often can't predict.

There's your temporary childhood, then you become an adult,
There are temporary hardships at the end of every month.
There are temporary friends you had that you never talk to today,
There are temporary moments when you just need to get away.

There's temporary schooling, until you graduate,
There are temporary problems that we all have to face.
There's temporary sickness and temporary good health,
The only thing not temporary is where you'll spend eternity after death.

My Mother's Residence

I wish I could support the employees, because they don't get paid that much,
To compensate for their compassion or their gentle caring touch.
The time they spend with patients, I couldn't begin to tell,
The many steps they take each day and care that's done so well.

They leave their homes each morning, their own problems stop at the door,
Realizing the things they'll see today, the heartbreak they will absorb.
They kindly get all patients dressed, then up and out of bed,
Then take them to the diner, making sure they all get fed.

They pass out all the medicines, take them back to their room,
Their work really now begins, with dust rags, mops and brooms.
Then they change all the linens, do their laundry too,
You'd have to see it for yourself, to appreciate all they do.

They comfort that aging mother, when Alzheimer's shows itself,
The things they witness daily is a life of living hell.
They offer so much hope to that long forgotten dad,
Since his family no longer has the time for him that they once had.

The things we all take for granted, as simple as going to the store,
These things are now impossible, since some can't walk anymore.
Yes I wish I could do something special for the staff at my mother's place,
Just to show my appreciation for every step for my mother they take.

I Loved You The Most

A teenage boy asked his mom, "How much do you love me?"
She replies "You were my favorite, out of all of the three.
With you I learned so much and did it with little sleep,
How to change a diaper, how to fix a skinned up knee,
How to make the perfect bottle, warm it up just right,
How to get a child to sleep, when he wants to sit up all night.
You taught me so many things, like how to be a good mother,
And that my son makes you unique, special above the others.
You were the first I ever held, the first I taught to walk,
The first time I was a mother, the first I taught to talk.
You were the first one I ever loved, the first to ride a bike,
There's no doubt about it, you're most important in my life."
A ten year old little girl asked, "Mom who do you love the best?"
Mom replies, "Of course it's you, I love you better than the rest.
You were the precious little girl, I prayed to have one day,
So between you and your brothers, you're my favorite I have to say.

In your eyes I could do magic, I could master anything,
Put pigtails in your hair with ribbon in blues and pinks.
In you I see my own self, when I was a little girl,
So now you know why that makes you, my favorite in the world."
A five year old boy asked his mom, "Which kid do you love more?"
She replies, "That's so easy to answer, it's you that I adore.
By the time you came into my life, I knew just what to do,
If I had to make a choice, no doubt it would be you.
You were so special, with you mothering came with ease,
By then I had mastered all the things that you would need.
You'll always be my baby, yes my darling little boy,
So out of all the others, you brought me the most joy."
"I loved you the most", a mother tells all three,
Each child lives thinking, they're as loved as they can be.
Never telling each other, what their mother had confessed,
They never doubted her love for them, because she loved them all the best.

Drama

Why do people love drama, guess I'll never understand,
They long to cause trouble, every moment that they can?
They can't wait to make a mountain out of a tiny molehill,
Come on folks grow up, is it really this big of a deal?

They run and tell this one and that one tells someone else,
When in reality, they ought to be ashamed of themselves.
They make things much worse than what they really are,
Drama is ridiculous, it can hurt a tender heart.

There can always be drama in any given relationship,
Instead of tolerating such, they need to get a grip.
Drama, drama, drama, engulfs their daily lives,
To me drama is a word that I wholeheartedly despise.

I think drama's even worse with that office personnel,
Some folks can hardly work for the gossip they must tell.
By the time it gets around to the employees at every desk,
The truth by now is gone, yes that would be my guess.

People need to get along and keep their tongues quiet,
Stay out of useless drama and everything will turn out right.
If good news could only travel, half as fast as the bad,
There'd be a lot less drama in the world, me for one would be so glad.

Siblings

We share the same last name and the same mom and dad,
Share thousands of different stories that only you and I could have.
We share the very same color of eyes, that's Carolina blue,
We even pull for the same team, it's UNC for me and you.

We share the same love for music, guess it was in our DNA,
Since our dad's a musician, we quickly learned to sing and play.
We share the same morals, we believe in the same God,
We share the same work history, for years shared the same job.

We've shared a million miles together, mostly in the same car,
Traveling the same highways to sing and play guitars.
We've performed at the same night clubs, shared the same stage,
We share the same talent that God graciously to us gave.

We share the same hair color and the same caring heart,
We both get up early, that's how our day starts.
We share the same type of blood, the same love for family,
Yes, siblings share the strongest bonds, especially you and me.

Things Money Can't Buy

There are many things in this world that money simply just can't buy,
A mother's gentle touch or that sparkle in someone's eyes.
A friendship that's lasted thirty years or a marriage sixty plus,
Or a relationship that's filled with, honesty, love and trust.

You just can't buy a healthy kid or an aging parent's life,
You can't buy true happiness or the air you need to survive.
There's no price tag on God's scenery, He paints like none other,
You can't buy the closeness between a sister and a brother.

Neither can you buy a clean conscience but you sure can get it for free,
By doing good deeds in life and being the person you need to be.
You can't buy compassion, you either have it or you don't,
It's great you can't buy someone's heart, some people's you wouldn't want.

You can't buy a child's laughter or that smile on their face,
The greatest things in life are free, like a hug, a kiss, an embrace.
The most precious, expensive and most important things in life,
Are the things that no amount of money could ever ever buy.

Good And Bad In Everything

There's good and bad in everything and summer time fits that list,
Even with temps in the 80's, it all comes down to this.
Especially for the people living down in the south,
Gnats, mosquitoes and bumble bees, swarm your face, your ears and your mouth.

There's so much extra work that's involved when it is hot,
Mowing the lawn, that dreaded weed eating, those hanging flower pots.
Pressure washing your home then you gotta restain the deck,
Remembering all you do in the summer that in the winter we easily forget.

You have to repaint the fence and then rake up all of the leaves,
Clean out all the gutters then clean those dirty eaves.
Put wood chips around the bushes and around those flower beds,
Pamper all of those flowers, remove the leaves that's dead.

Rake up all of that pine straw, that seems to never go away,
Constantly washing your car on any given summer day.
Trimming all of the bushes that isn't done when winter is here,
Cleaning out your closets, making room for summer gear.

Now on the other hand, in the summer you have more fun,
Picnics, walks, a day at the pool, when all of your work is done.
The beach is always inviting, especially when it's scorching hot,
So is the mountains, out of the two it's the coolest spot.

Down here in the south, summer often stays way too long,
Especially when it's 100 degrees, you start wishing those days were gone.
After a few long sweltering months, summer finally goes away,
Cooler temps begin to ease in, we all enjoy those days.

Next we all pray for snow and hope for once they predict it right,
Longing for snow to fall, throughout the day and into the night.
We like to see Old Man Winter arrive, we love him more when he leaves,
There's good and bad in everything and that you best believe.

Bucket List

Do you have several things that's still on your bucket list,
Things you've longed to do, things you don't want to miss?
Things you hope to accomplish, long before you die,
Or have you waited too late in life to even care to try.
Was a trip to Hawaii ever on your bucket list?
You put it off and put it off and never had time for this.
Did you ever want to ride one day in a hot air balloon,
But now that you're older, that adventure seems so doomed?
Did you ever wish to walk the entire Appalachian trail,
Or just see how far you could go, even if you failed?
Did you ever want to take a month or two long cruise,
And when it was actually possible, the last minute you refused?
Did you ever want to sleep on the beach the entire night,
Listen to the sea gulls, as they passed right by?
Did you long for a road trip, with no destination in mind,
Just pack some clothes, jump in the car and see how far you could drive?

Was visiting Graceland ever on your list or maybe Dollywood,
A trip to the Holy Land, and stand where Jesus once stood?
Was seeing the Eiffel Tower ever on your bucket list,
Or have season tickets for the Tarheels, me for one would have liked this?
Did you ever wish all you had to do was stay home and write all day,
Or learn to play a guitar, like the late Chet Atkins once played?
Did you ever want to learn to swim but the water you seemed to fear,
Or learn to drive a straight shift but was afraid of the clutch and fist gear?
Did you want to go to college and live that college life,
Instead you opted to raise a child and be somebody's wife?
Did you ever really desire, to see the Vatican Museums in Rome,
But looking back over your life, the only place you've been was home?
A bucket list sometimes is long, with nothing ever scratched off,
Often between work and raising kids, these desires just get tossed.
It's never too late to fulfill a dream or mark an X through things done,
No matter what anybody tells you, you're not too old to still have fun.

Everything I Am, I Owe To You (My Parents)

From the way I clean my house, to how I iron my clothes,
How I water my roses, from that old garden hose.
The way I make snow cream, even though yours is much better,
I way I hold a pencil, the way I make certain letters.

The way that I sleep at night, all curled up in a ball,
Our preferred seasons, are spring time and early fall.
From the way that I say grace, before every meal that I eat,
The way I always pray, each night before I go to sleep.

Everything that I've done well in this life of mine,
Came from your influences, to always do things right.
Every good decision that I have ever made,
I learned from the very best, great advice you always gave.

I got this tender heart from you but often it lead me to trouble,
But I wouldn't have it any other way, I wouldn't want a heart like some others.
The compassion I have for others, well that came from you too,
So did my abundant supply of patience, even my eyes of Carolina blue.

The way I raised my only child, I did it just like you,
The disciplines, the groundings, the spankings and that unconditional love too.
The way that I respect my elders with yes sirs and no ma'ams,
The way when I believe in something, I kindly stand my ground.

The good I see in others, when in reality they're kinda bad,
But it's all because they didn't have the kind of parents that I had.
So everything that I am today or everything that I'll ever be,
I owe it all to you and I'm thankful God gave both of you to me.

Before Technology

Way back in the 60's, we didn't have a cell phone.
If you wanted to talk, you used the one that hung on the wall,
Or just stop at a gas station, or the local corner booth.
Just pop in a dime, then talk as long as you needed to.

There wasn't such a thing as a thirty second email,
You had to mail your letters that was slower than a snail.
The same applies for paying those normal monthly bills,
Yes things have surely changed a lot since I was a kid.

As far as entertainment, you played outside all day,
No matter what the weather was, cold, sunshine, snow or rain.
You could actually opt to watch that three channel TV,
In total black and white, there was no such thing as HD.

Cable wasn't heard of and neither was satellite,
Rabbit ears with tin foil made the picture clear and bright.
There was no such thing as DSL, that hadn't been designed,
There wasn't any internet or social media of any kind.

There wasn't any Pac-Man, Angry Birds, or Donkey Kong,
Mario, Street Fighter and arcades, at that time hadn't come along.
There wasn't any Cabbage Patch Kids, Transformers, or Legos,
No Glow Worms, no Ninja Turtles, no Barney and no Gizmo.

Our games consisted of Marbles and of course those Pick- Up Stix,
Silly Putty, Hopscotch and Jump Rope, that gave us all a fit.
Gumby and Pokey, the View Master and Reels,
Play-Doh and Hoola-Hoops that gave all the kids a thrill.

There wasn't a GPS that could tell us how to go,
Instead you used a paper map, those directions were so slow.
How we ever managed in life, to live before technology,
From now until eternity will remain a mystery to me.

How Poor Are You

How poor do you think you are, do you ever sit and ponder,
About the things you don't possess, I bet you often wonder?
How rich do many others, always appear to be?
They have the best of the best, material things they never need.

They drive the finest cars that are made these days,
With the highest grade of technology made in Japan or the U.S.A.
Their cars all come with leather seats, those fancy back up lights,
The colors are often a sight to see, that shiny never fading kind.

They have a built in GPS, a stereo that rocks,
Yes, you can see them coming for many many blocks.
The mansion they live in, it's at least a quarter mile,
The clothes that's on their backs are always the latest styles.

Your home like mine is modest, humble and down to earth,
You're just what folks call middle class, you've been that way since birth.
While they have those costly lights, to decorate their lawns,
You sit on the front porch in peace, as the stars shine on and on.

You have the whole horizon, theirs is a well-lit patio,
They only own purebreds, that's not allowed to go where they go.
So the very next time you think, that you're really poor,
Remember if you count all of your blessings, could you really ask for more?

A Day in The Life Of a Home Health Nurse

At 6 am each morning, you stumble to the coffee pot,
With a long day ahead of you, making sure you haven't forgot.
There's a 9 o'clock meeting, telling you things you already know,
Like wash your hands often and with diabetics, check feet and toes.

Measure wounds each visit, document each thing you do,
Dot those I's and cross those T's before you think you're through.
Do a thorough assessment, ask patients about new meds,
Especially the ones in the window sill or the ones beside their bed.

The meds in the cabinet, the bottles lying on the floor,
And after you're through looking, I'll bet you'll find some more.
Pay attention to patients with Unna boots, CHF and HTN,
The psych patients at Woodhaven, your cycle never ends.

Ask patients about their pain levels, on a scale of one through ten,
And if they've had a fall, you'll need to fax that in.
Educate the care givers, they'll need it once you're gone,
The meeting is now over, you'll see more patients on your way home

You appear to have a hard shell but your heart, I've seen through,
By all of your caring ways and the little things that you do.
You'll call a Dr. in a New York minute, talk smack if he doesn't do things right
Like when he orders the wrong mattress, you'll put up a fight.

I remember you telling a Doctor, "Did I order a swimming float,
Or did I order a 4 inch gel, this patient needs it you know?"
You've put food on patients' tables with your money, you bought their meds,
And each night you pray for them, as you lay down your head.

You ask God for patience and to let each patient see,
Not only are you their nurse but a friend to all indeed.
You've touched a million lives, seen patients go from weak to strong,
Of all the nurses I've ever worked with, you're the BEST I've ever known.

How Many Times Can One Heart Break

The heart can be so tender, yet undoubtedly ever so strong,
No matter the amount of times it breaks, it continues ticking on.
It's got to be the toughest organ in anyone's body by far,
Since it handles so many wounds, wrapped up in several scars.

It breaks watching an aging mother revert back into childhood,
Yet it keeps right on beating, exactly the way that it should.
A heart can be ripped out easily, when words are spoken in anger,
Or when you see your once true love, become a total stranger.

When your teenage daughter slams that door and walks away,
And you don't hear one word from her, day after day after day.
A heart breaks in an instant, anytime death is involved,
It seems you spend forever, crying and questioning God.

Even when a friend betrays you, your heart forces you to still care,
It keeps on reminding you of the good times y'all once shared.
When a wife's heart is shattered by her husband's cheating ways,
She swallows all hurt and pride, her broken heart makes her stay.

I wonder how many times, one heart can withstand a break,
And still survive all of the trauma, it seems to always take?
But one thing is for certain, yes one thing is certainly true,
One heart can endure all hardships, all the pleasure and all the pain too.

When Strong Is Your Only Choice

Realizing how strong you are can come as quite a shock,
Strong always becomes reality, when strong is all you've got.
Even when the teardrops fall and pour down like falling rain,
Strong you still need to be, therefore strong you still remain.

Carrying a heavy burden can so often take its toll,
Even with the strongest, the most powerful and the bold.
Hiding all of your emotions, daily keeping it deep inside,
Everyone swears you are so strong, not realizing the tears you cry.

Keeping it all together, for the sake of so many others,
Your dad, mom, daughter and niece, your sister and your brother.
Being the rock they depend upon, your only choice is Army strong,
The last thing they need to see is you're not tough down to the bone.

Yes, being strong can be difficult but sometimes you have no choice,
When so many rely on you to be their strength, their guidance and their voice.
Somebody has to do it, I guess God thinks it should be me,
Therefore I willingly give it all I have and pray I'm all that I should be.

Sadly I Cry For me

I don't actually cry for my mother since she don't know what's going on,
But boy do I cry for me because I'm really not that strong.
I don't cry when she don't know me, I'm use to that by now,
Still it rips my heart to pieces, whenever she cries or frowns.

It's like she's now living, her life in an empty shell,
And if she remembers at all, it's often so hard to tell.
She never calls me by my name, in fact no words does she speak,
You have no idea what it does to me or how I feel helpless and weak.

I cry for me when no one's around, to watch my teardrops fall,
So many think I'm Sampson, I think I'm not that tough at all.
Others see me smiling, joking around and acting the same,
They should see me when I'm alone or when I call upon Gods name.

Yes in all honesty, I really put on quite a show,
Folks would be surprised, God how little do they know.
I cry for many others too and the daily things I see,
Hard to admit but so very true, yes sadly I cry for me.

Patience

Patience is a virtue, that's what the Good Book tells,
The more patience you have, puts you one step farther from hell.
Patience is born within and very seldom is it acquired,
Still you need to practice this word, to avoid that roaring fire.

Patience helps you hold your tongue and not speak out in haste,
Or say those can't-take-back words, which would be a major mistake.
Patience lets you tolerate more than so many others would do,
It also helps you keep your cool and to always think things through.

Patience can so easily destroy another's temper in many ways,
Mainly by just staying calm, no matter what they choose to say.
Patience is another fine quality, freely given by God above,
That teaches us endurance, composure and Heavenly love.

The amount of patience you have, in that heated state of anger,
Keeps the fire from escalating, keeps you more out of danger.
Keeping yourself in control, saves a thousand moments of regret,
You can take that to the bank and your last dollar you can bet.

Yes patience is even-tempered, an honorable God given gift,
Life is so less stressful, if you've been blessed with this.
So pray each day for more patience, make this change in your life,
However don't expect to have true patience overnight.

Being A Single Parent

While being a single parent, it's always a double-duty job,
It all comes down to you, all problems you must solve.
There's no "Go ask your moms" or" Just go ask your dads",
Sometimes it goes smoothly, other times it's rather sad.

Many times a single mother works two jobs sometimes three,
Just to put food on the table and supply everyone's needs.
They must check each child's homework, each and every night,
Try to raise them properly, make sure they turn out right.

Often a single dad works from sun up until sun down,
Even though he would like to be, most times he's not around.
He tries to talk to the kids at night, answer questions that's on their mind,
For example, "Where is mama, do you think we will see her sometime?"

"Daddy does she loves us, what did we do so wrong,
 Why did mama leave us?" and the questions go on and on.
Often single parents, have too much on their plate,
Not knowing all of the challenges, each day they have to face.

"Daddy do you still love her, would you give her another chance?"
"Mama whose gonna dance with me, at the Father-Daughter dance?"
"Who'll teach me how to drive a car, teach me to throw a ball?"
"Will mom be there to console me, when all my teardrops fall?"

"Who'll give me away mom, when I walk down the aisle?"
'Who will fix my hair dad and make sure I look just right?"
"Do you think mama would be proud, of who I am today,
I wonder if I cross dad's mind, in any kind of way?"

Decisions that adults make, affect a child in many ways,
You really need two parents, especially nowadays.
So when you want to venture out among your mid-life crisis,
Make sure your kids are not the ones left to make the sacrifices.

Unseen Angels

Everybody in the world has them, although they may never know,
They're often in unseen places, at your job or on a lonely road.
The one that seems to have your back, no matter the situation,
Who willingly goes to bat for you, no matter the occasion.

To that friend that fixed my car and wouldn't charge me any labor,
He said, "You never know one day, it may be me that needs a favor".
To that caring office manager, who lives in the real world like me and you,
Went out of her way to help me out, when she really didn't have to.

To the kind of boss we all should have, she would fight tooth and nail for me,
To me they're all unseen Angels and that I truly believe.
That stranger that stopped and helped me out, the time my tire was flat,
"No charge" at all he said to me, "I was glad to help with that".

I'm engulfed by thousands of Angels, I witness this each day,
From the kindness I see in others and their ever so caring ways.
God looks out for His own, in ways where we can't see,
I'm blessed with God's shield of protection that's always surrounding me.

There's Hope For The Brokenhearted

There's hope for the brokenhearted when out of reach it may seem,
Although at that very moment you'd like to give up on everything.
If you had your preference, you'd likely stay in bed all day,
Lay there just wishing, that your loneliness would somehow fade.

Deprived of any understanding, desperately trying to just hold on,
Hating the annoying sound of that ringing telephone.
Not bothering to set an alarm clock since you're not going anywhere,
Calling off work sick for days, not caring if you're not there.

Going too many days being secluded, too many nights without any sleep,
Can't even recall the last time, you sat down at a table to eat.
Never turning the lights on, there's nothing you care to see,
Staying in total silence, no radio, no comp, no TV.

Mad at the world because they're happy, while your world is a total mess,
When friends try to console you, you really couldn't care less.
Nobody hurts as bad as you and that you truly believe,
Not sure how long that it will take but one day you will surely see.

That mending a broken heart is never an easy task,
Trust me when I tell you, the pain won't always last.
There's hope for the brokenhearted, time really heals all things,
Down the road you'll realize, it wasn't as bad as it seemed.

It's Just What I Do

Taking care of old folks, well that's just what I do,
Farther down the road one day, I may need some help too.
I try to stay full of patience, showing them that I truly care,
The days they feel neglected, it's like I'm always there.

I also have a full time job and I rarely miss a day,
I have so many people that depend on me in every way.
No matter how I feel or what's going on in my life,
I'm always out there working, sometimes from five until five.

I visit my shut-in mother as often as I can,
Although I don't see God's reason, I try hard to understand.
I beg Him for a miracle, I also ask Him for a cure,
I pray He grants this request, at this point I'm not really sure.

I write what I think and feel and what I see others going through,
What you read isn't all about me, it involves many others too.
A friend or a family member, often strangers I really never knew,
Work, pray, visit and write, that just about sums up what I do.

Imperfect Vision

Am I really the only person, that has any vision in my home?
Although you wouldn't know it, I'm not the only one here that's grown.
Am I the only one that ever sees, that overflowing trash can,
Plates and glasses in the sink, along with silverware, pots and pans?

That basket of dirty laundry, nobody ever sees it but me,
And if the baskets empty, they're in the dryer just look and you'll see.
That empty roll of toilet paper, come on now give me a break,
We both know that you're gonna need it, since some things just can't wait.

The very same thing applies with, that same ole paper towel roll,
You actually see better than me, yet you still need to be told.
Let's talk about the vacuuming, nobody ever sees lint on the floor,
Or that the kitchen could use a scrubbing, we all could dust some more.

The dog could use more water, some food would be nice too,
If you would only take notice, there's so much that you could do.
I must have perfect vision, even though I'm three times your age,
I wonder how your house will look, one month after you move away.

Music

I love all types of music, let me back up and rephrase that,
I love country, gospel, rock, soul and pop but definitely not rap.
I love to hear a guitar player bending those six strings,
A drummer with perfect timing, to me that means everything.

I love to hear a piano player playing like Liberace,
Or someone tinkling those ivories, like Swaggart or Jerry Lee.
I love to hear a steel guitar whining way in the back,
But my favorite sound of all, has to be a tenor sax.

A country song is about cheating, someone always doing someone wrong,
Or how many beers it takes, to be incredibly strong.
A pop song is smooth and easy, like the Bee Gees and Andy Gibb,
Nobody can touch Gladys Knight and those harmonizing Pips.

Gospel songs are relaxing, they keep your life on track,
Once music is in your blood, there's just no turning back.
Rock songs of the 60's and 70's, some of the 80's too,
Make you wanna get up and dance to tunes, like "Blue Suede Shoes."

Elvis could sing them all, anytime, anyplace, anywhere,
"Love Me Tender", "How Great Thou Art", "Let Me Be Your Teddy Bear."
He could have sung the phone book and got a standing ovation,
I personally think he's the best singer, that's ever hit this nation.

God's Most Beautiful Painting

I look out of my front door and as far as I can see,
Once again God's painted a scenery that's so breathtaking to me.
The trees, the bushes, the barns, even that old ragged fence,
To me it's pure beauty, there's nothing prettier than this.

The well, the camper, the trucks, those empty parking lots,
It's a painter's finest masterpiece, painted by the brush of God.
The light poles and the cable boxes, even that junky trash pile,
Chicken pens, that horse stable, to me it's a beautiful sight.

The trash can, the porch chairs and also my outside swing,
Even the neighbor's pig pen is now appealing to me.
The basketball goals, garages and that flower-filled boat,
Competitions for the biggest snowman, just so kids can gloat.

Even my Tarheel spin wheel that spins so freely on my lawn
Yes days like these are truly the best times I've ever known.
This stunning awesome whiteness fills my heart with so much glee,
This very relaxing atmosphere makes a southerner's day with ease.

I'm sure my friends up north think we've totally lost our mind,
Finding enjoyment in things they detest, snow to us is wonderful and fine.
I could sit on the porch all day that is if it wasn't so cold,
Just to view God's painting, these days would never grow old.

We don't see a lot of it, therefore we go crazy when it falls,
To us it's a fun-filled paradise, yes we southerners have a ball.
The out-line of a simple bird feeder and the snow covered mailbox,
I am 100% positive that nobody can out paint God.

Second Chances

I believe in second chances, since everyone makes mistakes,
Wouldn't you want another chance if you were in their place?
That guy that went to prison for selling illegal drugs,
Now he has his act together and gives praise to the Lord above.

The teenager that got pregnant, now raising a baby all alone,
Even though this is all so new to her, she's determined to be strong.
The man that lied and cheated on his faithful wife of fifteen years,
He's now realized all of his mistakes, begs for forgiveness with heart felt tears.

The lady that got fired when she failed to show up for work,
She now knows that it was wrong, there should be another chance for her.
The woman that chose a man or drugs over her own little girl,
The regrets she has daily, I'm glad I don't live in her world.

That drunk driver that one day took the life of a teenage kid,
His life is now in shambles, each day living with what he did.
The guy that walked the streets, day after day he would steal,
Looking for a way to feed his family, remorse each night he feels.

The child that was disrespectful, saying things she didn't really mean,
She's apologized over and over, regretting her actions as a teen.
Some fences are hard to mend, too many people long to judge,
What if God didn't give second chances, that would be bad for all of us?

It's Just Who I Am

I keep things deep inside of me, I rarely let them out,
I don't have a temper, not one to holler and shout.
I ponder each decision in life that I ever make,
I always think things through, no matter how long it takes.

I strongly believe in God and strive to live like I was taught,
I know the greatest things in life are free and can't be bought.
I believe the way you treat others, your true colors will always show,
I believe whatever you do in life, you will reap whatever you sow.

I also think we all should work, as long as you are able,
I believe in saying grace, before I eat at anyone's table.
I think a child lives what they learn at home and examples I try to set,
I try to pray for everyone, although some names I may forget.

I try to be a good daughter, a good mother and a caring friend,
I try hard to please God, even though I fail now and then.
I'm as honest as they come, raised by the best mom and dad,
Sometimes I'm pretty happy, other times I'm indescribable sad.

Coca Colas and snow cream, well to me there's nothing any finer,
I'm proud to be a southerner, proud to live in North Carolina.
I pull for the Tarheels, yes those talented boys in blue,
If someone is ever in need, I try to do all that I can do.

I don't like to burden others with problems of my own,
I try hard to keep me together, I always appear to be so strong.
I make mistakes daily, I pray to be as humble as a lamb,
I just write what pops into my head, this is just who I am.

North Carolina, My Home

What a wonderful, incredible state, I was blessed to be born in,
Surrounded by good folks, great family and loyal friends.
Tobacco fields and cotton, as far as the eye can see,
Peanuts, sweet potatoes, soybeans, corn and lots of wheat.

The view here is amazing, from the mountains to the lakes,
The sound of the waves at the beach, salt water makes my day.
There are Pine trees, Christmas trees and Dogwoods everywhere,
Beautiful red Cardinals, flying in the warm Carolina air.

Awakened by the chattering of bluebirds, implying spring is near,
Hot summer days telling me that many fun-filled days are here.
We have winters that rarely consist of sleet, snow or freezing ice,
And even when predicted, the weatherman is seldom right.

Most of us believe in working and we also believe in the Lord,
We drive Toyotas, pick-ups, Chevys, Hondas and Fords.
We either pull for the Tarheels, Duke or N.C. State,
Yes I love North Carolina, to me there's no better place.

A Love That Alzheimer's Can't Even Destroy

She and I have been together, through all of the thick and thin,
The perfect love under any circumstance is guaranteed a win-win.
We were high school sweethearts and even on our very first date,
I knew in my heart right then and there, that she was my soul-mate.

She's stuck by me no matter what was going on in my life,
Still to this day I couldn't have found, a more faithful, loving wife.
We have been married sixty years, October will make sixty-one,
I can't recall one single thing wrong that she has ever done.

She's in a nursing home with Alzheimer's, a cruel and heartless disease,
I'd gladly take her place, if God would allow that to be.
Some people often ask me, "Why do you go see her every day,
She doesn't even remember you going?" I quickly turn to them and say,

"There's no doubt about it, if our roles were reversed,
She would never ever leave my side, she has always put me first.
I don't look at it as an obligation, it's undying love that is so true,
She may not know that I went today but one thing for certain, I do."

A Broken Heart

My heart is in shambles, can be devastating words,
Once you had perfect vision but now that vision's blurred.
It hits you in the heart and there's nothing you can do,
What once was your whole world has come down to only you.

It's like having a checking account, with no money in the bank,
A nice car that's insured but no gas in the tank.
It's like a good lead pencil that don't have a point,
Or a bar with no band playing, even in a bad joint.

It's like sitting in a deer stand, with no shells in your gun,
Broken hearts takes a toll, on each and every one.
It's like a Christmas tree with bows but it's missing the lights,
A dagger straight to the heart, especially on a lonely night.

It's like you're down with the flu and no one to get your meds,
It's like hearing words that's spoken but no words are ever said.
It's like going to the beach and all day long it's pouring rain,
It's like all you feel is numbness, loneliness and pain.

It's like going to a cook out and all of the food is gone,
Rooting for your favorite team, when they're barely holding on.
Life is full of disappointments, similar to those above,
No matter what a broken heart is still full of so much love.

The One That's Like My Daughter

The day that you were born, back in August of '79,
I'd longed for a little girl, secretly wishing you were mine.
I took you everywhere I went, dressed in the finest clothes,
To church, the park, the pool and of course we took Gizmo.

You were such a perfect child, didn't pitch a fit or cry,
You knew you had me wrapped, when you looked into my eyes.
No matter what you wanted, you knew I'd come through,
To grant you the latest toy or a new pair of shoes.

Then on graduation, I was the proud aunt that day,
Realizing my little girl had suddenly slipped away.
To the stage of adulthood, with many challenges in life,
The child I so adored was now someone's wife.

Your wedding day you were happy, me, well I cried,
Because God hasn't made a man, good enough for you in my eyes.
That October you gave birth, the child in you returned that day,
Seeing you in pain and tears, I had to walk away.

You've always been a healthy kid, that was until last year,
Heart surgery, then a stroke, nobody could calm my fears.
I prayed, "God heal her body, she's only thirty-three,
If you need a Hagan in Heaven, by all means, let it be me".

You may not be 100% but at least you're still alive,
Thanks to the grace of God and thousands praying day and night.
We have had our ups and downs, I've told you off a time or two,
But nobody could love you any more than I love you.

The "Mothering" That's Still In My Mother

My mother's a better mother than most that's still in good health,
She's just a middle class lady but her heart is filled with great wealth.
She doesn't cook or sew these days, she doesn't clean the house,
She sits all day so patiently and she's as quite as a mouse.

She no longer drives a car nor can she dress herself,
She's totally dependent on others but still she's the very best.
She likes anything you give her and in her own sweet way it shows,
Whether it came from Macy's or from the Five Below.

She's very soft spoken and glows with the sweetest smile,
She will share anything with you, just like a well-mannered child.
She no longer tells me what to do, she can only walk a few steps,
But the "mothering" part hasn't left her, I've witnessed that myself.

She takes her little baby doll and holds her gently but so tight,
Caressing her so tenderly and she rocks her to sleep at night.
She takes her soft blanket that sits there upon her lap,
And covers the baby doll up, holding her while she naps.

She's protective with her baby, you better not mess with her "kid",
The exact way she treated us, the same way as she always did.
Yes the "mothering" in her is still present, the loving care still remains,
Although so many things are different now, some things will never change.

Falling Apart

Are you the life of the party, while keeping your pain in?
Do you always wear a smile, no matter how rough things have been?
Would your co-workers and friends, just simply be amazed,
If they were in your shoes, even if only for one day?

Does everyone always say to you, "Oh you are so strong"
But you just can't lie to you, you know they are so wrong?
Yet you live each day, with love and joy in your heart,
Secretly hiding the fact, that you're about to fall apart.

Do you find yourself awake, where sleep once came with ease?
Do you wake up now crying, begging God to help you please?
Do you find yourself longing to just one day get away,
From where reality can't haunt you, each and every day?

Do you feel like an outsider, even though you still fit in?
Do you still feel alone, when surrounded by family and friends?
Have you ever felt as if, any day now you'll come unglued?
What keeps you together is God and people praying for you.

These Hands

These hands have ran a set of those fast flying shuttle looms,
These hands have set off firecrackers, that went pow, pop and boom.
These hands have held an infant, with an apprehensive touch,
These hands have given to others, although I don't think that I did that much.

These hands have worked in tobacco and I'll add at a very young age,
These hands have held a book, as I flipped from page to page.
These hands have been scarred, cracked, cut and dry,
These hands have consoled several kids that weren't mine.

These hands have held a microphone and I must say it was one of the best,
These hands have played a piano, from churches to bars I must confess.
These hands have played many instruments on a professional or make-shift stage,
From "Love me Tender", "Old time Rock and Roll", to "Amazing Grace"...

These hands have fed me and others, brushed my teeth and combed my hair,
These hands have washed my body, been folded many times in prayer.
These hands have fastened several buttons, zipped many pair of jeans,
These hands have ironed my clothes, ironed many other things.

These hands have clothed me and tied several pair of shoes,
These hands have put socks on others, they've even tied a tie or two.
These hands have held a puppy, hugging him after he left his mother,
These hands have played softball, with family, friends and co-workers.

These hands have embraced my daughter, held her close to my heart,
These hands have changed thousands of diapers and signed many report cards.
These hands hugged my child tightly on her graduation day,
These hands dried my tears, when she walked across the stage.

These hands have been sticky, clean, dirty and full of paint,
These hands have removed several spots and those set in grass stains.
These hands have cleaned my home and made beds every day,
These hands have held the wheel, while driving on various highways.

These hands have held a Bible and the hymn book in a church,
These hands have kept me busy, they're my strength when I'm at work.
These hands have wiped the eyes of the elderly living all alone,
These hands have helped many people and strangers I've never known.

These hands have held a grandmother, as she drew her final breath,
These hands protected a child, when they were scared to death.
These hands have touched a mother that was once so full of life,
These hands have held a dad, when on his knees to God he cried.

I believe these hands were given to me by God to help another,
And when I touch His face, it will be a touch like none other.
So use your hands wisely, let them always be willing to help,
Because when you're helping others, you're also helping yourself.

Soldiers

A little boys dream, when he's about eight years old,
Is to be like his daddy and walk on foreign soil.
To dress up in army clothes, with heavy equipment and gear,
He could hardly wait to join, approaching his eighteenth year.

His mother with uncontrollable crying, yet she's ever so proud,
To see the choice her son made, although she cried out loud.
His dad takes her hand saying, "He just wants to be like me",
"Everything's gonna be okay, just you wait and see".

Upon the young boy's departure, he instantly becomes a man,
Finally things become so clear, all things he once didn't understand.
He shakes his daddy's hand and holds his mother so tight,
Trying hard not to let her see, the tears that's in his eyes.

He waves goodbye to siblings and to his very best friend.
Yes today he's all smiles and laughter but every now and then,
You'll see him glance at his mother, trying hard not to let it show,
She's the one he hates to leave, the one he'll miss the most.

It's All In A Lifetime

When she takes her first steps, with that smile upon her face,
It makes you ever so glad, that you were in the right place.
When he starts to school and begins to play tee ball,
You're overwhelmed with pride, as his little body gives it his all.

When she has those sleep-overs and your house is a total wreck,
You're the one that's stuck with, cleaning all ten little girl's mess.
When he goes camping overnight, in woods that are dark and cold,
You pack blankets, drinks and supplies, to accommodate tenfold.

When she becomes a teenager, your nightmare suddenly begins,
You reminisce about the days, when she thought you knew everything.
When he gets his license and you're a total ball of nerves,
And when all that's on his mind is four wheels and a pretty girl.

When she goes out with a young guy, on her very first date,
You walk the floors and watch the clock, as the hours slip away.
When she walks across the stage on her graduation day,
Although you're not supposed to, you clap, cry and wave.

When she walks down the aisle, in her lovely gown of white,
Nobody in the world is as beautiful as she is on this one night.
It's all in a lifetime, you experience a lot more than you can recall,
But those precious once in your life moments are the most important of all.

Is there Anything Any Better

Is there any sound any sweeter than the laughter of a child,
Or raindrops on a tin roof as you're sleeping at night?
The sound of the birds chirping as they go their merry way,
Or the forecast predicting, mid -seventies day after day.

Is there anything any better than a warm tender touch,
Or the trust you see in a dogs eyes, knowing you're loved so much?
The smile you see on the elderly when you walk into their door,
Feeling a sense of gratitude, who could ask for anything more?

The weather on its best behavior while you're on your family trip,
Your first morning cup of coffee, smelling the aroma as you sip.
When that alarm goes off, getting that extra ten minutes of sleep,
Or answering your door as kids in costumes, holler Trick-or-Treat.

Watching your only son getting touchdown after touchdown,
The pitter-patter of little feet, what a precious sight and sound.
When the mailman made his deliveries, you didn't get bills that day,
When your paycheck is big enough to get everything paid.

Listening to your five year old, asking about Santa Claus,
Answering all of their questions, because in their eyes you know it all.
Watching a newborn sleep, the true meaning of being carefree,
Cokes stocked in the fridge or good ole southern sweet tea.

The days you don't need the heater or that pricey AC,
Nights of a clean conscience with your heart fully at peace.
Finding a few extra dollars, you didn't know was in the bank,
All of these taken for granted blessings, we have God to thank.

The World we Live in Now

Somewhere this very night, there's tears from a missing child,
Down in North Carolina, someone took another's life.
Out in California, they are marching for certain rights,
A bullied twelve year old girl in Florida, just committed suicide.

Up in New York City, there are people joining gangs,
Someone in Virginia robbed the local food bank.
In Chicago a teenager was robbed then shot to death,
A Georgia woman watched as her baby was shot in the head.

Out in Nevada, fire damaged homes and lives were destroyed,
Hurricanes tore up the East Coast, went by the name of Floyd.
The Oklahoma bombing claimed one hundred sixty eight lives,
In Orlando a young mother killed her only child.

An Arizona woman stabbed her boyfriend twenty-seven times,
In Mississippi, a child goes to bed hungry night after night.
An Idaho mother burned her little girl's remains,
A Phoenix baby left in a hot car until his helpless life was drained.

A Texas doctor was killed, murder for hire was the killer's goal,
In Ohio, three girls were kidnapped, man gets life without parole.
Twelve killed in a Washington Navy yard shooting, he also lost his life,
A New Jersey man killed his son and then he killed his wife.

Out in Colorado, rain destroyed thousands of homes, lives full of fear,
A Missouri priest producing child pornography, gets fifty years.
A musician in Raleigh, killed the mother of his two sons,
What's this world coming to, hatred, crime and misuse of guns?

Kitchen Beauticians

How many folks do you know that claim to be a beautician,
The shop they work from just happens to be their kitchen?
Now an actual beauty shop is often decorated kinda nice,
Then you have that homemade shop, take my word and think twice.

There are roosters on the wall, a fridge, stove, table and chairs,
People flock to their home for half priced beauty care.
You never see a shampoo bowl, nope the kitchen sink will do,
You get dye on your clothes, their floors and your shoes.

There's a box of hair color from your local dollar store,
Stained colorful towels, they've been used several times before.
There's always a bottle of shampoo, it don't matter what brand,
The same applies with the conditioner, even I don't understand.

You never see a styling station with mirrors and shelves,
These kitchen beauticians, I'm telling you, they're something else.
There's no hydraulic chair, straight back chairs work just fine,
The scissors they often use comes from the five and dime.

Well I had this experience and it was a few days ago,
I've been four colors since Sunday, what I am now, God only knows.
So I called a beautician, one with credentials on her wall,
I said "I can't take this humiliation, I'm at your beckon call".

She redid this head of mine and now I can honestly say,
This I might be able to live with for more than a few days.
So if you ever decide to get rid of your hair that's grey,
Don't use a kitchen beautician, you can't afford the price you'll pay.

What is Love

Love is so much more than just a little word,
Love is mostly silent but so often can be heard.
In a baby's laughter, a mother's touch, a tender warm embrace,
A six week old fuzzy puppy, a smile on another's face.

Love has no certain language, it's universal to all,
Love comes in all sizes, skinny, plump, short or tall.
Love has caring eyes of brown, blues and green,
This four letter word is the strongest word I've ever seen.

Love is patient, honest, faithful and so very kind,
Love can conquer anything, put you on the highest high.
Love is a feeling you feel through and through,
Love can melt the hardest heart with a simple, "I love you".

Love is at your bedside when death comes knocking on your door,
Love is God with open arms, to be in His presence forever more.
So many years ago, love was nailed upon a cross,
To prove the true meaning of love and pay the price at every cost.

Beauty in the Sky

Have you ever watched the sky when it seems so upset,
Thunder rolls, lightning strikes, you know what's coming next?
The rain starts pouring down, cleansing everything in sight,
Out comes the rainbow, what a beautiful sky.

Have you ever watched the sun rise from a back porch view,
Or noticed how the sky transforms the old day to the new?
The cool morning breeze blowing gently on your skin,
Giving you a relaxing, calming effect of peace within.

Have you ever watched the sun set when all you have is time,
Nothing clogging your thoughts, nothing weighing on your mind?
Just sit there in amazement, observing shades that blend,
Red, orange and yellows, what a soothing comfort they send.

Take time to see the sun rise then watch it set again,
Listen to raindrops falling on a roof made of tin.
Stop and smell the flowers, notice all of the different kinds,
Do all of this and more my friend while you still have the time.

My Brother

We've been through quite a lot, since we were little kids,
I often think about the crazy things we did.
We'd sing "Twinkle, Twinkle Little Star" and learned our ABC's,
We mended each other's broken hearts and cried over shattered dreams.

We broke our bones so many times, had cuts and skinned our knees,
Went swimming in the summers and learned how to sing.
We'd take mama's broom and daddy's picks and play a mean guitar,
We learned how to play the drums, beating on the dashboard of the car.

I blew the trumpet, the dog would howl, I'd make you hum the tune,
With all the music in our veins, guess mama's quiet times were doomed.
You cut your fingers to the bone, still learned how to play the steel,
With me pushing you not to give up and through prayers you were healed.

I watched you come so close to death, in such an awful way,
Bet I can tell you when it was, '91 on Valentine's Day.
I've seen you in just about every situation there could be,
The smiles, the tears, the hardships but in you I still believed.

We've both played a lot of music, at least a good forty years,
And no matter who I'm singing with, I always feel you near.
I can't think of a single soul that I think can play and sing,
Half as good as you can and that you can believe.

When I'm on stage without you, others only feel the space
I can't think of anyone that could ever take your place.
If I could grant just one wish that I knew would one day come true,
I'd wish all sisters in the world could have a brother just like you.

What We Could Learn

An old man was in room 203 fighting for his life,
His family gathered by his bedside, they began to cry.
He said, "I've lived a good life, two kids and a wonderful wife",
Then I saw the hand of God move and he began to smile.

The old man heard cries down the hall from the family of a little girl,
Praying, "God please spare her life, I'll do anything in the world."
He said, "Lord I've lived a life that's full and she is only eight,
If you'll let the Angels hold my hand, I'll gladly take her place".

Don't say you don't believe in God, I saw a miracle take place,
A dying child with no chance to live, now has a smiling face.
And God in all His mercy spared two lives that day,
To the stranger, who was willing to die for her and a child who laughs and plays.

Is there anything greater than a child's laughter or the humbleness of the old,
Or a heart that's filled with so much love, deep down in their soul?
Is there anything better than giving to a stranger, expecting nothing in return,
If we all lived like that old man, oh, the things that we could learn?

God Bless Old Folks

When I think that I have it bad and it seems I can't go on,
I look around and count my blessings that keep me oh so strong.
I see patients that are helpless with families that just don't care,
To offer a home-cooked meal or see the burdens that they bare.

A simple phone call is all it takes to make someone's day,
Stopping by to see them, as they go on their merry way.
A 50 cent get well card would put a smile on their aging face,
People so often forget, one day they might be in their place.

How would you like to lie in bed, can't move without some help,
Can't hold a normal conversation or even feed yourself?
Not sure if it's Monday or any other day of the week,
Just lay there waiting to hear a kind voice speak.

To wonder if you had five kids or was it just two,
Is their hair straight or curly, eyes brown or blue?
Is it Thanksgiving, or Easter or maybe the fourth of July,
Such a heart breaking vision will put tears in the coldest eyes?

Will they be alone again this Christmas, will the pain ever subside,
As they are longing for a miracle, falling asleep as they cry?
"Father, please forgive them, open their eyes so they can see,
Keep them safe and healthy so they won't end up alone like me."

Losing A Child Way Too Young

Today has started without you, yesterday I had no clue,
This would be the first of many tomorrows, I'll be spending without you.

Never more will you ride your bike or try to climb a tree,
Never play cops and robbers or build sand castles at the beach.

The fairy will no longer visit, the Easter bunny will never arrive,
No more playing at the pool or learning how to dive.

You'll never play hide-and-go-seek, never wish upon the stars,
Never say "Mommy, I love you", while falling asleep in my arms.

You'll never kiss me goodnight or be afraid of the dark,
Never go on another picnic or play at the park.

You'll never help me bake cookies, like we did on Christmas Eve,
The ones we made for Santa that I got to eat.

You won't rush to the window to see if Santa's on his way,
Nor will you try to sneak a peek, of Rudolph pulling his sleigh.

You'll never play with your baby dolls or play dress up in my clothes,
These are precious memories, ones I'll cherish the most.

So hold your child a little longer, it can end in the blink of an eye,
I pray that God will comfort any parent going through this tonight.

Why I Do What I Do

Sometimes I say there's got to be a better way to make a living,
Instead of riding the roads, seeing helpless people grieving.
Some people's daily lives is such a heart breaking mess,
Some a warm hello can cure, others are a train wreck.

One patient has no legs, diabetes also took their sight,
Another has bone cancer, in excruciating pain day and night.
One lady is totally paralyzed, she's so much younger than me,
A young man had a motorcycle wreck, he's only thirty-three.

Another woman's house should have long ago been condemned,
Her kids couldn't really care less or so to me it seems.
To get into another's house, you wade through grass two feet tall,
Another lady stays in bed all day, watching roaches crawl.

My goal each day is to make a difference in someone's life that I meet
Whether its job related or some stranger that's on the street.
To make someone's day much better, put a smile on someone's face,
I pray God keeps me humble and patient, so full of His loving grace.

I often go to sleep at night with all of this on my mind,
That's when I talk to Jesus, my direct Heavenly phone line.
I thank Him for His blessings and for the good health that I'm in,
When morning comes, I ask God to help me do it all over again.

New Year's Resolutions

As New Year's Day is approaching, many resolutions will be made,
We try so hard to keep them, often they last for just one day.
On our yearly never kept list, I think that I can name a few,
Of things that I believe could help us all, if we took the time to do.
Don't ever drink and drive and sitting alone don't drink too much,
Keep both hands on the wheels and don't be in such of a rush.
Count all of your calories, if you want to stay in shape,
Get out of bed on time so you never have to be late.
When the ball drops at midnight, put your cigarettes down,
Wear a much happier face next year instead of your worn out frown.
Stop all of your cheating, remain true to your spouse,
Make your dwelling a home instead of an ordinary house.
Stay out of the bars every night, spend more time with your family,
And just like the Army quotes, "Be all that you can be".
Set aside some time for you and stop living in the past,
Try to manage stress much better, believe in things you know will last.
Do a lot more exercising, go find a better paying job,
Never wear a proud look, stop being that sarcastic snob.

Stop borrowing from Mr. Peter just to repay Mr. Paul,
And if you decide to say "I do" then truly give it your all.
Be kinder to your neighbor even kinder to your enemies,
When you have a few extra bucks, give to the local charities.
Improve your relationship with that aging mom or dad,
Give God all of the glory and praise for all that you have.
Stop all of your whining and complaining every day,
Attend church more often and never ever forget to pray.
Never go to bed angry, stop holding that year long grudge,
Don't look down on others, always be careful not to judge.
Stop all of your procrastinating, go ahead and get things done,
And in everything that you attempt, try hard to have some fun.
Stay away from useless drama, let your life be filled with peace,
Let your mind overrule your heart, never give up on your dreams.
Always trust your gut feelings, let go of things you can't control,
Love with everything you have, willingly give your heart and soul.
Always treat your fellow man like you want someone to treat you,
If each of us would do all of the above, we'd be a better person too.

My Grandmother

I never called her grandma, she was always "Bibbie" to me,
To this day I really don't know how that name came to be.
She was the best southern cook in good ole Carolina,
Chocolate cake to die for, nothing to me was any finer.
The best cookies and pies and those mouth-watering jacks,
Reminiscing her sweet aroma, always takes me back.
To precious memories of her that I will forever treasure,
Just knowing this "Lady" was an honor and great pleasure.
She was kind and soft spoken, like an angel from above,
She was a great mother with a heart pure as a dove.

Since my dad's an only child, we never had to compete,
With any nieces, nephews or any other types of peps.
You could eat on her floors because she was just that clean,
Nothing was ever out of place and she ironed "everything".
Now when I say everything, you would actually be shocked,
Curtains, sheets and pjs, why she even ironed my socks.
She had the greenest thumb of anyone in the south,
If she had planted a tooth pick, I bet something would have started to sprout.

She took us for swimming lessons down at the city pool,
She never thought about dropping us off because she was old-school.
She sat in that hot car, always keeping us in sight,
If anyone had tried to harm us, she would have put up a fight.
She often read her Bible and prayed the way one should,
She also went to church on Sundays whenever she could.
She truly only wanted the simple things in life,
A roof over her head and a decent car to drive.
In the forty years I spent with her, she was surely one of a kind,
Loving memories of her forever embedded in my mind.

When God called her home, I fell upon my knees,
Questioned His decision, my heart full of begging and pleas.
Then I realized that she's much better off than you or me,
She now resides with Angels, right where she wanted to be.
She will never feel another pain, never shed another tear,
Never will she be lonely, she has nothing left to fear.
So God made the best decision, you know He's always right,
And one day in the future, I plan to walk right by her side.

These eyes

These eyes have witnessed a masterpiece from the greatest hands that paint,
The most perfect rivers and oceans, the beautiful Ohio lakes.
These eyes have seen the sunset on the Carolina shores,
Where waves touch the sun, leaves you yearning and hungry for more.
These eyes have seen roses, the prettiest flower of them all,
Magnolias, daffodils, carnations and perennials that stand so tall.
I've seen the Tennessee mountains that seem to touch the sky,
Hills, valleys and ridges, the most astonishing sunrise.
These eyes have seen winding roads that seem to never end,
Some gravel, some dirt, others mostly paved, yet something different around each bend.
I've seen the hottest summers and winters with ice and snow,
Fall and springtime with pleasant weather that's the seasons I love the most.
These eyes have seen sleet and this thing we call black ice,
In the south before you venture out, you just might wanna think twice.
These eyes have seen a robin making her babies a little nest,
Skillfully gathering materials from natures finest and very best.
These eyes have seen those gorgeous trees, along numerous interstates,
Pines, oaks and redwoods, all colors, sizes and shapes.

These eyes have seen houses with a million dollar price tag,
A falling shed on the highway, dwellings with shutters that sag.
These eyes have seen the sunshine and days of pouring rain,
Humidity that's unbearable, the destruction of hurricanes.
These eyes have seen tornadoes rip someone's world apart,
I've also witnessed the kindness in a stranger's heart.
I've seen puppies being born and the homeless going without,
It often makes you wonder, what the human race is all about.
These eyes have seen miracles performed each and every day.
The sight of God's presence simply takes your breath away.
These eyes have seen the innocence through the eyes of a child,
Hatred in adults, sadly, none to my surprise.
These eyes have witnessed the birth of a very special little girl,
I vowed to teach her the difference between the good and bad in this world.
These eyes have seen the elderly, so humble yet so alone,
Families have forgotten them, they're now living in a nursing home.
God's painted this whole world with such effortless grace,
But I wouldn't trade the things I've seen in the south for any other place.

One of Tarheel's Best

You get up after five phone calls and work from nine till nine,
Take at least two hundred calls per day, trying to keep us all in line.
You take referrals, handle complaints, audit charts, then go online,
To keep Tarheel updated on all the where's, when's and why's.

You make sure we've all had our shots and dates we have to meet,
Make out all the schedules and all that's done in between.
If someone is out of work, it's you that jumps right in,
Getting the patients covered, like they're your next of kin.

You listen to all of the grumbling, all of the good remarks too,
You always try to help us all, in everything that you do.
And when the State comes knocking, it's you that answers the door,
Assuring us it's a piece of cake, we've all had a slice before.

You tell us all, "Just do your best, the way you do each day,
The state will see you through my eyes and a lot of good they'll say."
Of all the people I've worked with, you surely surpass the test,
Making you, Jessica Richardson, one of Tarheel's very best.

Other books published by the author are :

Inspirational Poetry By Southern Chicks
by: Beverly S. Harless and Carol J. Hagan

© 2014 by Carol J. Hagan. All Rights Reserved.
ISBN-13: 978-1500951658

Made in the USA
Charleston, SC
11 November 2014